A Christian's Guide to Investing

A CHRISTIAN'S GUIDE TO INVESTING

Managing Your Money, Planning for the Future, and Leaving a Legacy

DANNY FONTANA

Revell
Grand Rapids, Michigan

Published by Fleming H. Revell
a division of Baker Publishing Group
P.O. Box 6287, Grand Rapids, MI 49516-6287

Printed in the United States of America

Library of Congress Cataloging-in-Publication Data
Fontana, Danny.
    A Christian's guide to investing : managing your money, planning for the
future, and leaving a legacy / Danny Fontana.
        p.   cm.
    Includes bibliographical references.
    ISBN 0-8007-3058-5 (pbk.)
    1. Investments—Religious aspects—Christianity. I. Title.
HG4515.13.F66 2005
332.6—dc22   2005008144

To my wife, Mary, who makes this side of eternity loving, and to my friend David Chadwick, who introduced me to Jesus Christ, this book is lovingly dedicated.

No investment program should be undertaken without a thorough discussion with a financial professional in which all appropriate personal financial details are revealed and considered. Investing is a highly personal and unique endeavor. All appropriate discretion should be exercised. No investment advice or financial planning strategy should be implemented without consultation with a professional financial advisor. This book is not intended to replace that process.

CONTENTS

1

FROM THE PENTHOUSE
TO THE OUTHOUSE—
AND BACK AGAIN

The Power of Talent Investing

I'm a "been there, done that" kind of guy. Most people who know me would say that I'm successful, at least in terms of net worth. The benchmarks for those conclusions have lost their appeal for me. I've learned that it doesn't much matter how big my house is, how expensive my car is, or how fast it can go from zero to sixty. My jeans don't have to be Calvin's, and my scent can be plain soap and water.

Maturity might have something to do with this de-emphasis on material wealth. As I got older, impressing folks got to be less important. I saw that there wasn't much point to making more money just to make more money. The stuff that money acquires offered little comfort during times of distress. There had to be more.

I spent many years relying on my own ability to find out what "more" was. I started my journey as a poor kid growing up in Endicott, New York, then emigrated southward during the Vietnam War years to settle in Charlotte, North Carolina. After some difficult times, I ended up on television and radio and acquired some modicum of celebrity. Mine was a kind of Horatio Alger story. Some people thought I "had it all." This book is about setting that notion to rest and offering you a financial blueprint that allows you to avoid my mistakes as you benefit from my professional experience as an investment counselor for the last twenty years.

In 1985 I went broke. That's right: flat, stone-cold broke. Not only did I have zero money, I didn't have a job or the prospect of one. In fact, with me in control of my business life and my personal finances, this financial wizard managed to personally run up a debt of $400,000. Not bad, huh? Calling the shots myself, I blew 400 large on a business that failed miserably.

At one time I owned nineteen shoe stores in four states. I called them Shubooties stores (sounds a little hokey now, but it worked in the '80s). My concept was to sell designer ladies' footwear for one price: $6.88. When I opened the first store in Monroe, North Carolina, in 1981, women figured out that this was a pretty good value, so they bought a lot of shoes. I opened a second store, and a third, and a fourth. Before you could say "personal guarantee," I owned nineteen stores. I had taken nothing and turned it into $4 million in annual revenue.

I thought I was the next Sam Walton. Like most human beings, when the business appeared to be successful, I thought I had something to do with it. Of course, when it all headed south, I wondered how God could do that to me.

The reality is that the success came from the Lord—and so did the failure. Obviously he needed me to be humbled to bring me to him. So he allowed me to lose $400,000.

I was thirty-five years old. I remember thinking that half of my life was over. So I made a decision: I didn't want to sell shoes anymore. I also didn't want to travel.

The question then became *What do I want to do?* That's a question I would urge everyone to ask.

Somewhere I had read a quote that always made sense to me. It went something like this: If you can't make your hobby your work, you will never go to work.

That forced me to ask a few more questions. What were my hobbies? Although I had an affinity for golf, that wouldn't allow me to pay off the debt (unless I was Tiger Woods, which I obviously wasn't). And the debt had to be paid. That was not an option.

Reading had also been a hobby. I always bought copies of the *Wall Street Journal* whenever I was in an airport. I didn't understand everything I read, but I still read it.

In 1982 I had gone to visit a boyhood friend. I had been trying to sell him a Shubooties franchise. Our meeting was set for early morning, so he invited me to a breakfast meeting with several of his friends. These ten guys got together once a month to talk about the stock market. They pooled their money, made decisions about what to buy or sell, and then went to their regular jobs. This was an epiphany for me.

When I returned home, I started an investment club that later became known as Group Ten Investments. Stocks became my hobby. I devoured everything I could read about the investment business, for a couple of reasons. First, I loved it. Second, whenever you get ten guys together for an investment club, it's difficult to get them to agree on whether they want McDonald's or Wendy's french fries, let alone what stock they should purchase. I rapidly figured out that I seemed to have some talent for leading their investment decisions.

So what was my hobby? Stock research and investing. Did stockbrokers make a lot of money? I suspected they did, which would allow me to pay off that looming debt. Would anybody hire me as a stockbroker? I had no idea.

I was broke. I had no formal financial training. I hadn't even graduated from college. Now I was faced with a new question: Why would anyone trust me with their money? After all, I had just gone broke.

The investment firm handling the Group Ten account was J. C. Bradford and Company, a firm that later merged with Paine Webber and then UBS Warburg. With a definite sense of trepidation but an equal sense of "How could I possibly be any worse off than I already am?" I dialed their office. To this day I can't believe they said yes.

On October 31, 1985, I reported to work as a stockbroker in training. I still owed $400,000, and my training salary amounted to $2,000 a month gross before taxes and deductions. While I tried not to look up at the mountain of debt facing me, I was acutely aware that if I had, Kilimanjaro would have been staring back at me.

At least I had a job with predictable money coming in. It wasn't much, but it was steady. What next? How do you pay back hundreds of thousands of dollars on two grand gross per month? The answer is: one day at a time.

During those first years as a broker, I started teaching investment classes at the local community college at night. That meant working from seven in the morning until ten o'clock at night three or four days per week. Weekends were consumed with preparing for the next week's class. In retrospect, it was fabulous training.

I could write another book on the specifics of how I paid that $400,000 debt back and how I guide other people to pay their debts. I don't want anyone to think it was easy. Most assuredly it was not. However, it was worth it (although you can be sure I don't want to do it again). Fortunately, the Lord allowed me to address the adversity, and he provided a way. I now know all things are indeed possible through the Lord who strengthens me (Phil. 4:13). To me those are not just words from the Bible; they are a living reality every day of my life.

How do I know that it was the Lord who did it and not me? Because there can be no other explanation. Quite simply, on my own, I could not have paid that $400,000 back in six years. Therefore, he must have done it.

The harsh reality is that too many of us are really bad at managing money. We don't understand budgeting, borrowing, lending, investing, or saving.

God blessed me with the ability to make a buck. Over twenty years ago I used that ability to acquire meaningless junk. Now I think the Lord is telling me to teach other Christians how to be prudent with money so we can serve the greater good for his glory. In the years since 1985 I have been managing money as a sales manager, a branch manager, and now as the senior partner of Triune Capital Advisors, LLC, a full-service brokerage firm. Prior to that I served on the Investment Advisory Committee for Interstate/Johnson-Lane. For nine years I also hosted "The Danny Fontana Show" on WBT radio in Charlotte, North Carolina. So I'm not a novice at giving financial advice.

First and foremost, however, this book is an attempt to teach the art of managing money using biblical precepts. Throughout the chapters I will suggest that you follow the advice in the parable of the talents: *invest* God's money (see Matt. 25:14–29). Don't hide it in your mattress, bury it in the backyard, or place all of God's gifts in a savings account. Be good stewards of God's blessings.

This book won't be a textbook. God's Word took care of the instruction manual. I will simply use real experiences from my life and some of my clients' lives to demonstrate the mistakes most people make and then apply principles of Scripture to solve the problems.

People ask me today, "What is the source of your optimism?" The answer should be obvious. Planning is important, but trusting in the Lord is more important. If you believe it, the Lord will provide.

2

HOW COULD I BE THAT STUPID?

The Seven Basic Mistakes Investors Make

I used to begin the investing class I taught in a North Carolina community college by talking about the seven basic mistakes investors make. The men and women in the class were from all walks of life. As in the parable of the talents (see Matt. 25:14–29), they had all been given different resources. Some had a minimal amount of money to invest—the one talent. Others had the equivalent of three or five talents. And as in the parable, how they handled these resources would make the difference. Saving a certain amount per month could insure their opportunity to retire successfully if they avoided these seven mistakes.

Mistake #1: The Failure to Set an Investment Objective

I always started the class with the same question: "What do you want your money to do?" Invariably people responded with the obvious: they wanted their money to make money. However, that response is incomplete since it fails to take into consideration *how* they wanted their money to make money.

An accurate investment objective identifies the clients' circumstances. Investors might want their money to grow over time. They might want it to provide a tax advantage. The investors may or may not want their money to provide an income, and, believe it or not, at one time a legitimate investment objective was to lose money intentionally in order to provide a tax write-off!

The point is that most people don't spend any time at all thinking about who they are and where they are in their lives; as a result, they under- or overestimate their ability to tolerate risk. Risk, you see, is the big, bad boogeyman in the investment world. Because of that, one would think that investors would consider it.

Let me give you an example of how an inaccurate investment objective can mess up an investment plan. Suppose that an investor needs to make money grow over time in order to enjoy a proper retirement. This investor sees a 3 percent certificate of deposit (CD) advertised in the newspaper and invests $10,000. Let's see if this money grows over time by doing a quick mathematical analysis:

Interest at 3 percent on $10,000 annually	$300.00
Taxes paid on earnings at 37 percent	−111.00
Purchasing power lost due to inflation	−200.00
Return from investment	− 11.00

How does that make you feel? Nauseated? Yet I'll bet at one time or another in your investing life, you bought a

CD thinking it was a prudent decision. This is the classic example of failing to identify what it is you are trying to do and then matching your money problem to the proper investment solution. I want to make it clear that nothing is wrong with buying a bank certificate of deposit. It's just not a growth vehicle. A CD is designed to provide safe, reliable income, and it does that extraordinarily well. *The investor needed growth but bought reliable income.* Classic!

The situation is compounded when you place the wrong kind of investment in the wrong kind of account structure. In the preceding example, the investor would have compounded the problem by buying the certificate in an IRA account. Failing to provide growth is the first mistake. The second is failing to provide the tax advantage the growth would have gotten had you bought it in the proper account.

So it becomes most important for people to know what their investment objectives are. Investments are generally categorized as:

- **Growth**: These assets are intended for use way down the road. A forty-year-old person investing for retirement at age sixty-five would want his or her assets to grow. The best example of a growth investment is the stock market.

- **Income**: These assets are generally intended for immediate use and therefore should pay you something for owning them. They should have little or no risk to the principal associated with them. The best example of income investments are Treasury bills, bonds, notes, CDs, and money market accounts, although there are many, many others.

- **Tax Advantaged**: These assets are intended to provide a tax advantage to the owner. The growth or the income offers some form of tax relief. Examples of tax advantaged investments are fixed annuities (a life insurance contract that pays you a fixed amount of interest for a fixed period of time) and municipal bonds. Variable annuities (where the interest and the period of time both fluctuate, depending on the stock market) represent an example of tax advantaged growth investments.

- **Speculative**: These assets are intended to provide a high rate of return quickly. Most people confuse speculative investments with growth investments. The difference between the two involves the amount of time you hold the asset. A stock owned for growth would be held for ten, twenty, or thirty years—or longer.

   The same stock owned for speculation might be bought and sold the same day. The main feature of a speculation is that investors can lose most of their money very quickly. Of course, they can also make a significant percentage of return in a short time. Because of this high risk/reward scenario, investors should never place more than a small percentage of their assets in this category. Examples of speculative investments would include options, derivatives, raw land, and aggressive growth stocks.

Novice investors need to ask themselves one question before even attempting to invest: What is this money for? The successful answer to that question averts this first common mistake.

Mistake #2: The Failure to Put a Plan in Place

Common wisdom goes like this: people don't plan to fail, they fail to plan. Nowhere is that more true than in the world of investment. I call it getting to Waxhaw.

Waxhaw is a rural town about twenty miles east of Charlotte, North Carolina, where I live. If you have never been to Waxhaw and you would like to go, how would you go about getting there? You would ask for directions.

In order to go from Charlotte to Waxhaw, all you need do is drive straight down highway 16 east out of Charlotte and, provided you don't turn off the road or run out of gas, you will arrive smack dab in the middle of Waxhaw, North Carolina. It's the same with investing. You find out where you are, determine where you want to go, draw a map to get there, follow those directions, and *voila*, you end up where you wanted to go.

Let me demonstrate it like this. Let's suppose that you have $10,000 in cash, that you are thirty years old, and that you want to have $1,000,000 by the age of sixty. Some of you might think it's impossible to have this much money when you retire. "I'm not wealthy," you say. "My salary is not in six figures. I only make $60,000 a year. That's just impossible." Not so. Follow my analogy. You are in Charlotte (ten grand), you want to go to Waxhaw (a million buckos), and you have thirty years to do it (highway 16). Here are the directions:

1. Start with $10,000.
2. Save $5,000 per year for the next 30 years.
3. Invest with a growth objective and get 10 percent on an average compound basis.
4. At age 60, you have $1,000,000.

Trust me, the math is correct. Now, what can go wrong? Let's take a second look at our road map:

1. You don't start with $10,000. (You are not in Charlotte.)
2. You don't save $5,000 per year for the next 30 years. (You can't find highway 16.)
3. You don't get 10 percent average returns. (You run out of gas.)

4. You don't have $1,000,000 at age 60. (You don't get to Waxhaw.)

Obviously, anything that interferes with your road map impacts your financial plan. Yet the net result is predictable for most investors. The map is correct.

However, most novice investors don't have the knowledge or experience to even think up the plan, let alone implement it. This is further frustrated when one does not know the proper vehicles to achieve the 10 percent rate of compounded growth. The one investment vehicle that has demonstrated the ability to compound at 10 percent over a long period of time is the stock market, period! That information alone scares most novice investors who view the stock market as a speculative vehicle rather than the growth objective it truly represents.

To really understand what I am illustrating, let's examine the concept of compounding money over time. Einstein called compounding the greatest invention of the twentieth century. Who am I to argue?

In order to understand compounding (paying on both the accrued interest and the principal), one has to grasp the theory of the "Rule of 72." Basically, take a rate of compounding, divide it into 72, and you know how long it will take for your money to double. Prudent stock market investing should yield average returns of 10 percent over time. Taking into consideration the Rule of 72, at 10 percent, money doubles every 7.2 years (72 divided by 10).

Let's use our getting to Waxhaw analogy to demonstrate the power of compounding. Just take the $10,000 that we started with and compound it by the Rule of 72 over our thirty-year period of time. It looks like this:

Start	$10,000
7 years later	20,000
14 years later	40,000

| 21 years later | 80,000 |
| 28 years later | 160,000 |

Oh, that Einstein! Not just another pretty face. You can readily see how you can accumulate a million dollars if the original grubstake of only $10,000 (without the additional savings of $5,000 a year) turns into $160,000, can't you?

Mistake #3: The Failure to Consider Taxation and Inflation

Earlier, I gave you the example of the 3 percent certificate of deposit and demonstrated what happens to gross returns when you apply the banditry of taxation and inflation. Three hundred dollars disappeared, eaten up by those two robbers.

Interestingly, taxation is considered the more insidious of the two. However, investment professionals have long known that inflation is the more severe threat. Taxes are only paid on investment returns if you have at least made some money. Inflation robs you of purchasing power on assets whether they are going up, stagnant, or even going down. Let's look at this robber first.

Inflation

Since 1946, inflation has averaged about 4 percent per year on a compounded basis. Let's go back to our Rule of 72. Inflation works just like an investment return. In this case the Rule of 72 tells you how long it takes for an item to cost twice as much. If the inflation rate is 4 percent per year, you would divide 72 by 4, which equals 18. Therefore every 18 years, goods and services cost twice as much, with an average 4 percent rate of inflation.

21

Think about the price of your first car. Now think about the cost of the same item today. My first car was a red Ford Mustang that cost $2,500 in 1965. Today a Ford Mustang can cost upwards of $30,000. Folks, that's inflation, and it's relentless.

The importance of the inflation argument gets to the heart of growth dollars. Investors have to grow dollars *throughout their lifetimes* in order to keep pace with their purchasing power. Inflation doesn't stop because you retire.

In my investment practice, I have seen too many people fail to consider stock market investments because they perceived them to be too risky. Their thinking is impacted by their loss of a paycheck once they stopped working. The reality is that most people will live fifteen, twenty, even thirty or forty years after they retire. Consider what inflation does to their nest eggs over that period of time. When they retired, thirty years ago, $30,000 in income was comfortable. Today, in order to have the purchasing power of thirty years ago, their income would have to total $97,000. That is how people on fixed incomes run out of money.

Inflation is why people need to have a portion of their assets exposed to growth for their entire lifetimes, unless, of course, Rockefeller, Kennedy, or Carnegie is in the bloodline. I'm not trying to be flippant about this. In my opinion, failing to account for inflation is one of the most fatal mistakes investors make.

Now let's look at that second robber: taxation.

Taxation

Taxation is an entirely different matter. Taxes are the price one pays to live in the United States of America. You can impact the effect of taxes by lobbying Congress. Think taxes are too high? Throw the bums out. You cannot do that with inflation.

This is not to minimize the importance of considering prudent tax strategies, like limiting capital gains by waiting for a cost step up or dollar cost averaging. Suppose that your father bought his house for $100,000, and when he died he willed it to you. Only now the house is worth $400,000. Because he willed the house to you, you get a *step up* in the cost basis. If you sell the house two weeks or so after he dies, you have no capital gain. But if he had sold it before he died, he would have paid tax on $300,000 worth of gain. We'll get into specifics about cost step up and dollar cost averaging in later chapters.

For now, know that a mistake is made when an investor needs money and so decides to sell a stock without taking into consideration the taxable effect, or when this investor takes a distribution from a retirement account without realizing the tax ramifications because that looks like an easy place to get money. Believe me when I tell you that hundreds of millions of dollars are burned by investors every year simply because they do not know the taxable impact of their investment decisions. That, folks, ought to be against the law.

We live in a great country. Taxes, while annoying, are the price for our freedoms. We should not under any circumstances try to evade paying our taxes. Notice that I used the word *evade*. Evading taxes is illegal. *Avoiding* taxes is not only legal but prudent.

Let's say you need $5,000 to pay some bills. You sell that amount of securities in your self-directed IRA account, not knowing that taking money out of a retirement account prematurely (before age 59½) carries with it a 10 percent tax penalty. The following April, your certified public accountant (CPA) or tax advisor tells you that you owe $500 in penalties to the IRS. You could have avoided the penalty in several ways. The point, however, is that most investors don't even know about the penalty. That's the flaw. You need

23

to ask about the tax ramifications of any strategy before implementing it.

Mistake #4: The Failure to Use Other People's Knowledge

We all need professional people in our lives. Yet none of us likes that fact. The reason? Professionals cost us money. For example, who likes to go to the doctor or the dentist? We know we need to, but we don't want to. First, we're afraid the dentist's remedy might hurt. Second, we know it might also be painful to pay a dentist's or doctor's bill. Yet we go to dentists and doctors because we perceive the need for medical advice. The average citizen knows that a doctor possesses more knowledge about disease than he or she does. In the end Joe Citizen is willing to pay a premium for that knowledge. Doesn't mean he likes it.

But if Joe gets sick, watch what happens to his perception. Worse yet, let Joe's wife or child get sick. All of a sudden, he doesn't mind the cost. All that runs through his mind at that point is, *Cure my loved one!*

The same analogy applies to lawyers. We all poke fun at lawyers. But face a judge one time and tell me who you want standing next to you. Accountants generally get no respect, unless you get a notice from the IRS requesting an "interview." Try to buy a house without a banker. We all need professional people in our lives, yet most of us try to avoid them.

It's even worse for financial professionals. A recent survey showed financial professionals rated just above used car salesmen for honesty and integrity. Ouch! What makes this worse is that people think they can manage their money by themselves. They have no perceived need.

The proliferation of no-load mutual funds, magazines, and infomercials over the last ten years has convinced people they don't need a financial background, education, or experience in order to be a successful investor. However, the years between 2000 and 2003 in the marketplace pretty much erased that error in judgment. The losses sustained by the individual investor after the market peak of March 2000 are staggering.

Human nature is an astonishing thing. Nowhere is that demonstrated more perfectly than in the world of financial services, and that is because of the two prevailing emotions that govern investors: fear and greed. I'll talk in depth about fear and greed when I discuss the business cycle in chapter 4. For now, know that people will invest when they are greedy but not when they are scared. Couple that with the knowledge that market prices are high when people are greedy and low when they are scared, and you get the mistaken buy high, sell low approach to investing that most people experience.

That is why individual investors need the benefit of other people's brains. Investors need to figure out which prevailing emotion they are operating under before investing. I'm oversimplifying the role of a trusted financial advisor, but for purposes of this discussion regarding mistakes, it's appropriate. Just know that it's a mistake not to seek good counsel before you invest a nickel in anything.

Mistake #5: The Failure to Provide for Your Estate

Do you have an up-to-date will drafted by a professional? We have all heard the horror stories about well-known celebrities like Elvis Presley whose wealth was devastated by Uncle Sam after they died. As I write this, the Congress is contemplating changing the estate tax in order to allow Americans to retain more of the wealth that has taken a lifetime to accumulate. However, they haven't done it yet.

In 1992 my father was diagnosed with terminal cancer. Being a financial professional who was aware of the horrible pressures placed on the family when a loved one dies, I asked my dad if he had his affairs in order. Was the house titled properly so that his widow-to-be would not have to endure governmental interference when the estate was settled? He assured me that he had taken care of everything and that the house, in particular, was in joint name with rights of survivorship.

Well, after he died, I found out differently. The house had to be re-titled with lots of wear and tear on my stepmother. I gain nothing by trying to figure out my father's motivation in lying to me. The point is that most people don't even know how to title their assets in order to insure a smooth transition. This mistake can cost your heirs a lot of money. More importantly, it puts your heirs through needless anxiety at a very stressful grieving time. Why do that to your family, especially when it can be addressed with the stroke of a pen?

Could this and other estate problems be solved at a minimum cost with just a tad of planning? You betcha. The techniques are not necessarily complex, but you will need some help to think through the issues. We will consider these techniques in chapter 9. For now, let's just say that the problem can be corrected by avoiding two of the seven common mistakes: a lack of estate planning and a lack of good counsel.

Mistake #6: The Failure to Diversify

Most people understand the definition of diversification. They might simplify it by restating the old credo, "Never put all of your eggs in one basket." While there is an element of truth to the statement, this doesn't help identify which baskets your eggs ought to be in.

Investment dollars fall into three different categories: safe dollars, growth dollars, and risk dollars. Here are the definitions:

- **Safe:** Can't lose. This investment won't make much return, but you won't lose principal either. Some examples include checking accounts, money markets, Treasury bills, certificates of deposit, and cash.
- **Growth:** You can lose the principal, but if you are prudent, you probably won't. I'll explain the role of prudence in an investment philosophy in chapter 6. The classic example of a growth investment is a portfolio of blue chip stocks.
- **Risk:** You can lose! Probably all your money and probably pretty quickly. Examples of risk dollars are speculative options and casino games.

A prudent investment plan would include the identification of these investment profiles and the percentage of ownership. For example, a young investor needs to be heavily weighted towards growth. Look at the difference age makes in the investor profiles in the box below:

Investor Profiles	
Young investor:	5 percent safe, 90 percent growth, and 5 percent risk.
Middle-aged investor:	20 percent safe, 75 percent growth, and 5 percent risk.
Elderly investor:	70 percent safe, 30 percent growth, no risk.

Obviously, each investor's profile is different because the profile reflects each investor's risk tolerance given his or her age. Every investor ought to know how and why his or her money is positioned, which can be seen by the Investment Triangle on the next page.

The Investment Triangle

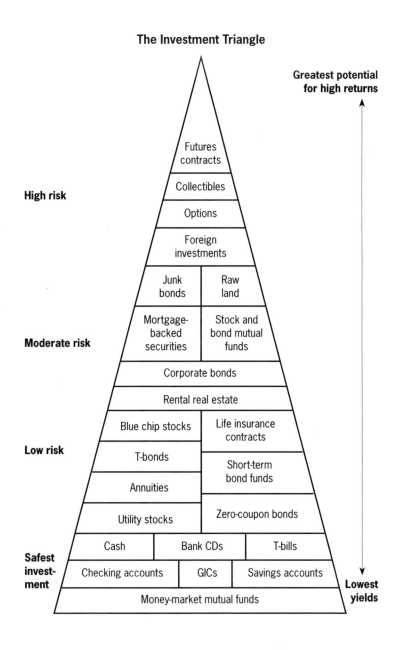

True diversification is probably the most misunderstood of all investment concepts. People oversimplify the process by not recognizing the sub-context within all investment categories. For example, investors might think they have a diverse growth portfolio because 70 percent of their holdings are in the stock market. Well, what if 100 percent of that 70 percent is in one stock? That flies in the face of diversity.

Similarly, five stocks are not enough. Neither are ten or twenty or thirty stock holdings. A recent study suggested that it takes sixty to seventy individual stocks spread across asset classes (like growth) to get the kind of diversification that mitigates risk.

One need only think of all those folks who held only Enron stock in their 401(k) accounts to understand what I'm illustrating. I don't care how much the company touted owning Enron stock; no employee who understood the concept of diversification would have been wiped out by the management's shenanigans.

Mistake #7: The Failure to Use Insurance Effectively

Most people buy the wrong kind of insurance for the wrong reasons and end up paying way too much for a product they may or may not need. Whenever I see someone under thirty years of age paying big monthly premiums for whole life insurance, I see someone who didn't do his or her homework. In order to make prudent decisions, investors need to understand what they are trying to accomplish by purchasing life insurance.

The first question I want an investor to ask is, "What are the proceeds from a life insurance policy intended to do?" For most people, life insurance proceeds are intended to replace income lost as a result of someone's untimely death. That is a legitimate reason to purchase life insurance, but that protection should be purchased with cheap dollars. What is the least expensive type of life insurance? Term. What is the most expensive type of life insurance? Whole life. The mistake occurs when investors confuse the two.

Young people in particular make this mistake. When I was twenty-six years old, my uncle worked for an insurance company and sold me a $250,000 whole life policy. Now, whole life takes half of my premium dollars to pay for death benefit insurance. The other half? The insurance company invests that, and folks, insurance companies are lousy money managers. In fact, they were so bad that during the 1990s they were forced to admit that rather sad fact and hire professional money managers to make the investment decisions for them. While that's better, their performance is still lousy.

The second problem with whole life insurance is the fees. Generally, insurance salesmen get paid their commission from the entire amount of the premium during the first several years. That delays the buildup of cash value. What the salesperson will show the young person is the significant cash value on a projected basis down the road. What the young person ought to be looking at is the guaranteed cash value (the amount of money this person could collect in five years or so). The difference is significant.

All of this can be made moot by examining the motivation. Death benefits ought to be paid with cheap dollars given the law of large numbers (the foundation upon which risk is measured by insurance companies). The younger you are, the cheaper your premium ought to be, since the lower likelihood of your death translates into less risk for the insurance company.

The logic of the argument against whole life comes into focus when you think about who has wealth in our society. Generally, younger people have not had time to accumulate wealth; therefore, their loved ones need protection in case they die suddenly. They need death benefit protection; they do not need the insurance company as an investment advisor. Older people have accumulated wealth and may not need this death benefit protection. They are self-insured, which simply means that if they die, their loved ones will have enough money or the ability to take care of themselves without leaning on the proceeds of a life insurance policy.

I should point out that I am not talking about investment life insurance products, like a variable annuity. That is a horse of a different color. The mistake principally involves paying high dollars for what could be a small dollar purpose.

So there you have it: the seven most common mistakes investors make. My guess is that most of you have made one or two or even all seven of these mistakes. The rest of this book is all about correcting those mistakes so we can be good stewards of our money.

But let's pause just a moment now and have you begin drawing an initial plan to get you from Charlotte to Waxhaw.

The Waxhaw Worksheet

1. Date when you need the money: _____
2. The number of years until you need the money: _____
3. Amount of money needed to reach Waxhaw (your goal): _____
4. Money already accumulated to reach Waxhaw: _____
5. Rate of return assumed for accumulated money: _____ percent (3 percent for CDs, 10 percent for stocks)
6. Money remaining to be accumulated: _____
7. Money needed to be saved annually at assumed rate of return: _____ (see below)
8. Money to be saved monthly (previous line divided by 12): _____

31

Okay, let's say that you want to accumulate $1,000,000 and you have thirty years to do it. Here's how:

Start with $10,000

Invest $5,000 each year for thirty years

Get 10 percent compounded return

You end up with $1,000,000. You need a special financial calculator to do this (like a Hewlett-Packard 12c).

  a. Enter 10,000 present value (PV)
  b. Enter 30 years (N)
  c. Punch in 10 percent interest (I)
  d. Punch in 5,000 payment (PMT)
  e. Punch in future value (FV)

3

LARGE CAP, MID CAP

Understanding Types of Investments

Maybe you have never invested in anything other than a savings account at the bank. If that's the case, here's an overview of what's available to you as an investor. We'll start with the least risky investment and proceed to the most risky. To keep things simple, we'll break investments down into only two types: fixed income and growth.

Fixed Income

Fixed income investments are characterized generally by a protection of your principal. In other words, you will hold these investments for a set period of time, they will pay you interest during that time, and then you will (presumably) get your money back at the end of the specified time. Let's look at the most common types of these investments.

Certificates of deposit. You buy these at the bank, and the competition for your money is generally pretty brisk. Some banks will use a CD as a loss leader trying to get you to deposit money in CDs in order to capture you as a customer. The theory is that once you have your money in the bank, you will never take it out. The interest on CDs is generally based on the overall level of interest rates, and they are typically low-yielding investments.

Treasury obligations. Treasury bills, bonds, and notes are offered by the U.S. government and are generally considered the safest fixed income investment vehicle. For that reason, they have very low yields. The difference between them exists solely in their holding periods. T-bills are sold with maturities of three, six, and nine months. T-bonds have holding periods of from one to five years, and T-notes are held over five years and go up to thirty years. Obviously, the longer the maturity the higher the interest rate, generally speaking, although there have been times when the "yield curve" has been inverted with the five-year rate of interest being higher than the ten-year rate of interest. Needless to say, those are interesting times. What makes these investments so safe is that they are backed by the taxing authority of the United States government. You are guaranteed to get your money back after the holding period by the full faith and credit of the United States of America—historically, a very solid guarantee.

Municipal bonds. These are generally the same as U.S. government bonds, but instead of being issued by the federal government, they are issued by states and municipalities. The interest paid for these securities enjoys the benefits of reciprocity. The federal government allows the states to raise money for their projects and keep the interest free from federal taxation. Once again, the interest rates are generally lower than other fixed income vehicles because of the tax advantage and the low level of risk resulting from the interest also being backed by the full faith and credit of the issuer. Since the states also have taxing authority over their citizens, "muni's" are viewed as very safe, although there have been some defaults.

Corporate bonds. These are fixed income investments issued by corporations. Obviously, the sounder the corporation, the safer the investment is deemed to be. A mature corporation (one that has been around for many years and paid dividends for a long time) will be viewed much more positively than will a brand-new company that pays no dividends. A company's finances and longevity determine their ability to repay their loan obligations. Various rating agencies make it their business to rate a corporation's ability to pay their interest obligations. You can determine this by asking for a company's "rating." Generally speaking, a corporation is deemed to be "investment grade" if they have a rating higher than BBB (triple B). Investment grades go from AAA (safest) to AA (less safe), A (less safe still), and BBB (least safe). Anything below triple B is labeled "non-investment grade" or "junk bonds." While junk bonds pay higher rates of interest than investment grade bonds, the risk of default increases with each quarter point of increase. So, buyer beware.

Government agency securities. These are almost as good as bonds issued by the federal government. Although they don't carry the guarantee that Treasury bills, bonds, and notes have by being backed by the taxing authority of the government, these agency issues are a pretty good bet since Congress will make certain they don't default. Remember the savings and loan deal of the mid to late '80s? Investors stood to lose billions of dollars in deposits, but Congress made certain that did not happen with the promise of the Federal Savings and Loan Insurance Corporation (FSLIC). Because these securities are not directly backed by the taxing authority, they are viewed as slightly riskier and as a result carry a higher yield. Many agencies issue such securities, and you generally can buy them from a broker. Here's a partial list:

Export-Import Bank
Farmers Home Administration
Federal Farm Credit System
Federal Home Loan Bank
Federal Home Loan Mortgage Corporation (Freddie Mac)
Federal Housing Administration (FHA)
Federal National Mortgage Association (Fannie Mae)
Government National Mortgage Association (Ginnie Mae)
World Bank
Small Business Administration
Tennessee Valley Authority (TVA)

Some of these corporations are owned by the government. That's why they are considered so safe. As always, you should evaluate the individual bond to see whether or not it might be right for you.

Mortgage-backed securities. Shortly after you get a mortgage, it is often sold to a federal agency, which repackages it in the form of a mortgage-backed security. You pay your bank, the bank gets a fee for collecting the payment, and the federal agency guarantees investors the interest and principal as it comes due, even if you are late with your payment. For the investor, a mortgage-backed security provides regular monthly income as it's paid by homeowners. The investor gets the interest plus a little of the principal each month. The breakdown of the payment (how much interest, how much principal) is broken down on the investor's brokerage statement each month.

Now, this can seem like a really good deal, but the investor has to be careful that the principal doesn't get paid down too fast. This can and does happen when interest rates are going down rapidly. This is a problem if you are spending the monthly income to live. When rates are going down rapidly, you could be getting fairly hefty monthly checks because the mortgage principal is being paid down faster than normal with all those folks out there refinancing their houses. Here's the really bad news: if they pay you back all of your principal and interest prematurely and you spend it, you have nothing left to reinvest. The investor knows these types of investments as Ginnie Maes, CMOs (Collateralized Mortgage Obligations), or REMICs (Real Estate Mortgage Investment Conduits).

Bond mutual funds. Buying bond mutual funds has some advantages, but it also has some caveats. First of all, buying bonds this way allows diversification, the choice of how you want the income paid to you, and lower commissions. However, the expenses can vary widely and can definitely impact the yield on your money, so study this product carefully before deciding to buy. Bond mutual funds also offer automatic dividend reinvestment so you don't have to wait until you accumulate enough money to buy individual bonds.

The thing that sticks in my craw about bond mutual funds is that they never mature. That means that you run the risk of your money never getting back to even. As a broker, bond mutual funds were possibly my least favorite investment. I saw too many people lose too much money too many times to feel warm and fuzzy about the investment possibilities, although I want to stress that for some people with very specific income needs, bond mutual funds offer the proper solution.

Unit investment trusts (UITs). These investments buy a fixed portfolio of bonds and hold them to maturity. These are different from bond funds which buy and sell bonds constantly and which never mature. UITs come in $1,000 minimums and can be very effective in their yields since yearly expenses are generally very, very low. The investor usually pays 4 or 5 percent on the front end as a sales charge, but over the long run, the fees for UITs are much less than bond mutual funds.

The advantages to UITs are: diversification, identification of the bonds in the portfolio, fixed monthly income, access to your capital if you need it, maturities (meaning you get your money back if you hold the investment for the entire length of the UIT), and the ability to choose from different types of income (including tax free). The main disadvantage is the same as with any bond-type investment: you can lose principal due to default or rising interest rates.

Growth

The two most common types of growth investments are stocks and mutual funds. Let's look at each.

Stocks

The best investment for growth is stocks. Investing in stocks means that you become a partial owner of that company along with a bunch of other people. Since you own part of the company, you own "equity" in that company. That is why stocks are often referred to as "equities." The shares you own fluctuate in value constantly because some people think the company is going to do well and others think the opposite, all at the same time. Remember this very important advice: as convinced as you may be that the stock that you buy is going to rise in value over time, somebody else is equally convinced of exactly the opposite. If more people think that the company should do well, the price of the shares will go up, and vice versa. The upside in stock ownership is limitless. A stock can grow to the sky, theoretically. The downside is defined—you can only lose what you paid for the stock. A stock cannot go below zero.

Certain rights are associated with owning stock in a company. You are entitled to quarterly reports, dividends, and voting privileges. The reports will tell you how the company is doing and how they expect to do in the future. You can also find out the company's vision or plans at the annual shareholders' meeting. If you ever get the chance to attend a shareholders' meeting, I urge you to do it. While boring, it is educational. For the most part, stock ownership rights represent a kind of rubber stamp approval of the company's executive plan since most people cannot own the percentage of stock necessary to make a meaningful voting impact on a company's policy.

The dividend right is a big, big deal. You can make money from stock ownership if the stock price goes up, but you can also make money by receiving the company's annual dividends. If the corporation makes money and the board of directors thinks it might be a good idea to declare a dividend, then you might get a quarterly check. Dividends are usually paid by well established, older, "blue chip"-type corporations that do not need all of their capital plugged back into their growth plans. During times of economic distress, a portfolio of common stocks that pays a healthy dividend can smooth out the ride for stock investors. For example, during the 1970s the stock market did very little in the form of appreciation. The Dow Jones Industrial Average went up only one half of a point in ten full years! However, by reinvesting the dividends, an investor could have earned an average of 12 percent compounded by buying stock at depressed prices during that decade.

Now, why does a company sell its stock? Because it needs the money. When a company sells its stock to the public for the first time, it's called an initial public offering (IPO). This is a very common practice when companies reach a point in their development where they can see an opportunity to grow but do not have enough capital in order to fulfill their vision. They sell stock to the public and use that money to buy other companies, pay down their debt, or build new factories. Shares in initial public offerings are tough to get. That's probably a very good thing since IPOs are risky. The money from the sale of the shares goes directly to the company after commissions to their investment bankers are paid. If a company needs more money to grow and they have already done an IPO, they can issue what's called a secondary offering. But most of the time, when you buy shares of stock, you are buying it from another seller and not from the company.

Remember my warning. When you buy stock, somebody is willing to sell it to you. Now, there may be a number of reasons for the sale of a stock. Perhaps the people selling it have already made a lot of money on it, or perhaps they need the money for other investment purposes. They might need to pay taxes or something else. Whatever the reason, you won't know why the person is selling. I don't think that you need to. What is important is the number of people willing to buy or sell their shares. When there are more people wanting to buy a particular stock than to sell it, the price of the stock goes up, and vice versa.

The most important thing for investors to comprehend is that stock ownership is no different than owning your own company. If the company does well, the stock of the company does well. That's the good news. The bad news is that investors can suffer a total loss of their investment if the company they own falls on insurmountable hard times. This risk of principal loss is mitigated by a couple of factors. One is the element of time. Generally, the longer you hold an investment, the smoother the risk ride. The other reason naturally follows the first: investing in mature companies rather than newer companies generally reduces the risk to your principal. Of course, all stock market investments involve risk to your principal, whether they be fully mature (blue chip) or in their infancy (aggressive). *Caveat emptor!*

Mutual Funds

I must confess an affinity for stock mutual funds for a variety of reasons. One is that by their very nature, they make the stock market viable for the average investor. Many people believe that stock ownership is only for the Rockefellers or the Carnegies. The advent of mutual funds prove that opinion false. Mutual funds pool many investors' money into a bigger pool and buy and sell stocks on your behalf for a fee. The mutual fund managers decide what to buy, how much to buy, and when to sell. This takes the research responsibility out of the hands of you or your advisor and places it squarely on the manager. Now you and your advisor get to sit on the same side of the table and assess the performance of the manager. I mentioned that fund managers manage money for a fee, so that gets me to my pet peeve: *there is no such thing as a free lunch*. People believe that no-load mutual funds (with no sales charge) are better than loaded mutual funds (with a sales charge) because somehow that means that they are free. While the no-loads are free of the upfront sales charge, they do charge an administrative fee to manage the money. In a lot of cases involving no-loads, the administrative charges are more expensive over a period of time than the upfront charges for competitive funds. What should be important to investors is the performance of their funds taking into account all fees and charges. Let me demonstrate it to you this way. What difference does it make if you paid 2 percent per year if the fund that charged you the 2 percent performed much better than a fund that charged you nothing? Focus on what's important—and in the world of mutual funds, the only thing that is important is performance.

41

Another major reason to consider mutual funds is the instant diversification that becomes available to you. Because the fund owns dozens or even hundreds of companies within its portfolio and you own your pro-rated share of the fund based on the amount of your investment, you own dozens or hundreds of companies.

The transaction costs are much lower with mutual funds. The mutual fund will pay lower commissions for its purchases and sales than you would on your own. That's an advantage.

Mutual funds are liquid. You can get in and out really easily. All it takes is a phone call to your advisor or to the fund directly, and bingo, you're done.

You can set up automatic investments, and the fund company or the brokerage company can draft your checking account on a monthly basis. How cool is that? This is the easiest way I know how to pay yourself first painlessly.

The fund reinvests dividends and capital gains into additional shares if that is your desire, or you can have them send you a check. Reinvesting allows you the "dollar cost averaging" strategy so critical to stock market success. Dollar cost averaging is a systematic program of buying stock regardless of price over time. For example, you buy stock for three months in a row at $10, $12, and $6 per share. Your average cost at $10+12+6 \div 3 = \$9.33$.

While mutual funds offer a great alternative to individual stock ownership, investors do need to be aware of some pitfalls. Owning one mutual fund does not accomplish the asset allocation objective necessary for portfolio management. In other words, although a large capitalization growth stock mutual fund (one that owns big, fast-growing companies) owns hundreds of stocks, it still only owns large cap stocks. To be truly diversified, the investor should also own small cap growth, mid cap growth, large cap value, mid cap value, small cap value, and international stocks. So the investor would best be served owning proportionate shares of mutual funds that invested in those different types of companies in order to round out the asset allocation.

Here's a great way of looking at a risk progression starting with the least risky and moving to the most risky. I'm going to use mutual funds as my investment vehicle. Here's what this progression would look like:

Money Market Mutual Funds
Fixed Income Mutual Funds
Income Funds
Growth and Income Funds
Growth Funds
Aggressive Growth Funds

While there are various and sundry other investment vehicles, this book focuses on bonds, stocks, and mutual funds and leaves the intricacies of limited partnerships, options, hedge funds, and so on to the more astute investor. The financial basics outlined here can put you well on your way to wise and productive investment.

4

WHAT GOES AROUND COMES AROUND

The Business Cycle

Let's pretend that you quit your job today to open your own business. How do you think you might feel? Do you think you might be just a tad apprehensive? Sure, you are probably exhilarated, but you also have to be a bit scared as you think about what you left behind. The 401(k) is gone. The medical plan is gone. The paycheck is gone. If the new business needed capital to get started, I bet your savings are also gone. Any way you look at it, this is scary.

Now it's a year later. No one would mistake you for a Rockefeller, but you are not starving either. You pay your bills on time. The kids aren't hurting for anything essential. You are starting to think this new venture of yours just might work. In short, your fear has been replaced by hope.

Five years later, you just left a meeting where the biggest bank in town has expressed an interest in loaning your business some money since you are seriously thinking about expanding into another location. You have been profitable for the last three years, with the last year being the best yet. You're the Superman and Godzilla of the business world. There is no one smarter than you. There may not even be anyone better looking. You, my friend, are bulletproof, and you cannot fail.

That chronology shows how the American business cycle is punctuated by three emotions: fear, greed, and hope. If you learn how to read those three emotions, you have a leg up on successful investing. And if you master the cycle, you will know when the odds favor stocks or bonds, growth vehicles or cash.

Business Cycle Basics

To introduce you to the business cycle, let me give you a tangible example of what it looks like in action. From 2000 to 2002, the stock market went straight down. People had their net worth trimmed in half. They saw their 401(k) become a 201(k). How did many stock market investors feel going into 2003? Scared, right down to their socks. That's fear.

The first half of 2003 saw the stock market rise over 20 percent on the Standard and Poor (S&P) 500 index. People's fear had been replaced by hope. They were still nervous about owning stocks but less so. But wait a few years. If the market continues to rise, investors will think the stock market can't go down. That's greed.

Isn't that right? Yet investors quickly forget this cycle. Now, here is something you need to write down. Until somebody repeals capitalism, the business cycle is here to stay. *When you are scared, buy stocks. When you are hopeful, hold those stocks. When you feel you can't lose, lighten up on your stock positions.* That, folks, is how you invest in the stock market, based on the business cycle.

Sir John Templeton, a legend in the money management business, started investing in the stock market at the dawn of World War II. At that time he borrowed $10,000 from his father-in-law in order to buy 100 shares of every stock trading on the New York Stock Exchange, for less than $1 per share! Sir John bought 104 different issues. In 1950 he started Templeton Investments, which he sold for a billion dollars in the early 1990s. That's the stuff of legends.

I had the opportunity to interview him for a television special I hosted called "Stock Market 101." I asked this legendary figure how he knew when to buy stocks. Here was his answer: "Danny, the time to buy stocks is when there is blood in the streets. No, that's not quite right. The time to buy stocks is when the blood in the streets is your own."

Put another way, *stocks are cheapest when your prevailing emotion is fear.* When every fiber in your being is warning you not to engage in the stock market, that's when you should consider that activity.

In all of my years of investing other people's money, I have never found a solitary individual who didn't intellectually agree with what I just said—yet could actually do it joyously, knowing it was the right thing to do. Even those who can buy at distressed prices are nauseated as they are doing it because of the prevailing sense of foreboding that overhangs bear markets.

The reverse is also true. During the decade of the 1990s, the stock market increased by 19 percent compounded annually. People were quitting their jobs and cashing in their 401(k)s in order to day-trade the market. That is the personification of greed. When people choose to behave in an imprudent manner, they generally do so due to the greed factor. So if stocks are cheapest when the prevailing emotion is fear, *stocks are the most expensive when the prevailing emotion is greed.* Tying the economic conditions to those two disparate emotions will enable investors to plot stock market strategy with some level of comfort.

Now let's look at the economic indicators that signal fear just over the horizon and those that signal greed. In order to master this phenomenon, an investor needs to know how to read the economic tea leaves. The successful navigation of the stock or bond markets begins by understanding that markets are predictive and to some extent self-fulfilling. Let's start by analyzing those economic indicators that factor into the creation of these two emotions.

Five Economic Indicators

These five economic indicators have a direct bearing on the American economy:

- the direction of interest rates
- inflation
- gross domestic product (GDP)
- the U.S. dollar
- the money supply

The Direction of Interest Rates

Any discussion of interest rates has to involve an analysis of the Federal Reserve. The "Fed" is the nation's central bank; the *capo di tutti capo,* the godfather, if you will, of all the nation's banks. The role of this central bank can be debated (and often is *ad nauseum*).

One school of thought renders the central bank as the *lender of last resort,* the place to go when there is no place else to go. The day after the stock market crash of 1987, the financial markets needed a place to turn to for succor and comfort, not to mention hundreds of billions of dollars. The then chair of the Federal Reserve, Alan Greenspan, gave the markets the liquidity they needed to continue to function. Notice that the markets did not go to the executive branch of the federal government. They went to the Federal Reserve. I see no clearer definition of a lender of last resort.

That said, the main role of the Federal Reserve is to try to keep the nation's economy on an even keel. This is done primarily by exercising control over "monetary policy," which is accomplished by infusing money into the marketplace or removing money from the marketplace. When times are tough, the Fed releases funds into the markets. This is called providing liquidity. When times are great, the Fed restricts the supply of money. The biggest tool for the Fed to exercise this monetary control (albeit not the only one) is the manipulation of interest rates.

Member banks borrow money from the Federal Reserve system when times are tough. (That's right. Your bank borrows money from the Fed.) They do this in order to meet reserve requirements. Let me simplify this just a bit.

After the Great Depression of 1929, when tons of banks closed their doors because they ran out of money, the Federal Reserve created a reserve system whereby all member banks in the system had to maintain so much cash on hand. To make sure that the banks complied, guess what? The Fed checked!

What if a bank wanted to make a loan of a million dollars to Joe Businessman, and Joe needed the money by three the next afternoon? (Let's assume Joe is good for the loan. If the bank doesn't loan him the dough, the bank loses money.) But if the bank loaned Joe the money, this bank would not have the cash reserve necessary to keep the Fed happy. So what does the bank do?

Bill Bank Chairman thinks, *I know. I'll borrow the money from another bank that has more cash reserves than it needs, and I'll pay*

49

that bank back right after the Fed counts my cash. The Fed is happy, the other bank is happy, and Joe Businessman and everyone else who borrows in the future will be happy. Of course, I'll be happy to pay a little interest to the other bank. After all, what are friends for?

That is called lending money on an overnight basis. The rate of interest charged between member banks on overnight loans is called the "discount rate." Who sets that interest rate? The Fed, of course.

How does this impact the economy? By keeping the amount of the reserve requirement low, banks have more money to lend. By keeping it artificially high, the banks have less money to lend. Want to speed up an economy? Lower the reserve requirement. Want to slow it down? Raise the reserve requirement.

What has this got to do with the direction of interest rates? The rate gets ratcheted up or down depending on whether the Fed wants to keep money tight or loose. Remember, the Fed sets the lending rate between member banks.

Member banks also borrow directly from the Fed itself. When a bank borrows from the Fed, the central bank charges interest to the member bank. This rate of interest is called the "federal funds rate." Lower the fed funds rate and a bank can attract more loans from their customers, since it costs the customer less to borrow. Raise the fed funds rate and fewer people will be anxious to borrow money. Whenever you hear a news flash—"The Federal Reserve has raised [or lowered] interest rates"—the reporter is talking about the fed funds rate.

The central bank can manage the money supply another way: the Fed can authorize the printing of more money. That's right, they can simply say, "Hey, crank up the printing press." How's that for power?

The Federal Reserve can also buy United States Treasury bills, bonds, or notes on the open market. That's still another way to keep the system awash in cash. Of course, if the Fed decides to sell these debt instruments, it takes cash out of the system.

So, in a nutshell, there you have the workings of the Federal Reserve. By controlling the supply of money in the country through the manipulation of interest rates, the reserve requirement, the printing of currency, and buying or selling on the open market, the Fed can either ratchet things up or down.

Those of you who thought the president is the most powerful person in the country now know better. The chairman of the Fed doesn't have to convince Congress of a thing in order to call the money shots. That's power!

So what can we make of an easing of credit by the Federal Reserve? What does that mean economically, and how can the proper prediction of the Fed's actions help you as an investor? Well, if you owned a business that had to borrow money, how would you feel about having to pay less for that money? Very good, I imagine, since you would have more money to invest in your business because you saved money on interest. Obviously lower interest rates favor businesses and help them to grow their profits.

Stock prices go up when investors expect that companies will make more money this year than they did last year. Consequently, lower rates generally point toward higher stock prices. The reverse is also true. Higher interest rates kill business profitability, which lowers stock prices.

So, as an investor, when do you want to buy stocks? When interest rates are expected to go higher, or lower? The key word in that last question is *expected*. The stock market anticipates the economic future. That is why things are often bleakest when the market is fairly optimistic about the future.

For example, the Federal Reserve lowered interest rates twelve times from 2001 through the first half of 2003. Yet the stock market performance was horrible during that time. The reason? Those interest rate declines needed time to translate into corporate profits. The first half of 2003 started to show that upswing in profits, and the market, while slow to respond to the first rate cuts, began to spring to life by advancing 10–12 percent on the Dow averages. By the end of that year the S&P 500 index finished over 20 percent.

Inflation

Inflation robs an investor of purchasing power over time. Therefore it is an economic indicator and a predictor of corporate profits. Consumers want to know that prices will be somewhat stable in order to feel confident about spending money.

One need look no farther than the following statistic to understand how important a happy customer is to the American economy. Fact: our combined confidence in the economy, translated into spending, accounts for almost two thirds of gross domestic product growth. Now, let that sink in for a moment. Two thirds of the nation's growth depends on whether you are comfortable enough to buy a car, a boat, a home, a suit, or a pair of pants.

Let's demonstrate this phenomenon with the tragic example of the events of September 11, 2001. When those planes flew into the Twin Towers, we stopped spending. Prior to that horrible event, the economy was emerging from recession. However, our fear short-armed this recovery. The prospect for top line sales growth hit the skids, and companies pulled in their spending. Capital expenditures completely dried up, and a downward cycle went into motion. No consumer spending meant no corporate spending. That caused job losses and a vicious cycle—one that was entirely predictable.

Two years later, after major combat in Iraq was over, some measure of consumer confidence was restored, and that triggered some capital expenditures by corporations. One might ask, What does any of this have to do with inflation?

The answer: higher prices depress consumer confidence. The knee bone is connected to the shin bone in so much of economic analysis.

When prices are falling, or at least not rising much, the consumer feels better about things. While it's true that buying can sometimes be triggered by higher prices (think about locking in a mortgage rate—if you think rates are going up, you will rush to get yours done), higher prices usually depress the stock market. Thus, the second economic indicator to watch is the direction of inflation.

Gross Domestic Product

An ideal situation is for our economy to progress slowly but relentlessly upwards. Gross domestic product is defined as the sum of the nation's goods and services. When the gross national product rises, the economy is said to be in expansion. If the growth rate declines for two consecutive quarters, we are said to be in recession. This is a critical concept to grasp. Politicians will do anything to avert recessions because presidents get fired during recessions. Just ask George Bush the first.

Looking at GDP gives us a chance to examine how economic indicators are linked. Lower interest rates give businesses confidence so that they will try to make money on borrowed money. That confidence translates into the willingness to hire more workers to make more products. More products keep prices stable. Stable prices increase consumers' confidence, so they spend more money. The knee bone is connected to the shin bone. When we spend more money, the nation's growth rate rises. When the nation's growth rate rises, presidents get reelected.

The same analysis needs to be done in reverse. Higher interest rates give businesses pause about borrowing money, spending money, or hiring workers. That means less product, and that translates into higher prices, which we call inflation. Too much money chasing too few goods—that is the classic definition of inflation.

Think of it this way. Suppose you own the only lawnmower in your neighborhood, and every lawn except yours is overrun with weeds and brambles. Everybody's property values are plummeting. Your neighborhood is pitiful, except for your verdant wonder. Your grass is neatly clipped; your hedges are crisply trimmed.

Now, all of your neighbors have a lot of money but no access to lawnmowers. They want what you have. What do you think your lawnmower might be worth? That is how inflation works. Give people the means to buy something but then restrict the availability of whatever it is that their hearts desire, and that means higher prices. Whether it be Cabbage Patch Dolls, Pet Rocks, Beanie Babies, or oil, the pricing process is the same.

Higher prices obviously translate into nervous consumers because no one wants to pay more than necessary. Think about how you might feel if you paid $100 for a cashmere sweater only to find it on sale the next day for 50 percent off.

Whenever one talks about the nation's growth rate, one has to dive into the perilous political realm that is dubiously called fiscal policy. One also has to contrast that fiscal policy (practiced by the politicians) with monetary policy (practiced by the Federal Reserve). The two are seldom compatible. When a president wants tax cuts, the Fed chairman may counsel Congress against it, and vice versa. So what's the truth? Who really knows how to manage the nation's money, the federal government or the Federal Reserve? And why should we even care?

Well, let's start here. Politicians, as a rule, don't know beans about money except how to spend it. Here's proof. We ran deficits in the United States for over thirty years. In other words, we spent more in government expenditures than we collected in tax dollars. If you did that for three months, you would be in deep, deep trouble. The government did it for over thirty years.

What happened as a result? Anybody go to jail? Not to my knowledge. And why not? The politicians get taxpayers, investors, and other countries to make up the shortfall. The credit of the United States's system allows us to sell our government debt all over the world and take in tons of cash as a result. We finance our overspending by selling government bonds, notes, and bills to investors and foreign institutions. Don't you wish you could do that?

Realistically, everyone knows how to cure a deficit. You either take in more money or you spend less. Ideally, you do both until the deficit is gone. You might get a second job and cut up your credit cards until you can see the light at the end of the tunnel. That's your solution to a deficit, and a good one it is.

Now let's translate what more income and less spending sounds like to a politician: higher taxes and less service. There isn't a politician in the free world who doesn't know that this platform is the end of his job security. So let's look at the traditional two-party system and see how the politicians would solve the deficit spending that plagued America for thirty years.

Generally speaking, the Democrats would have taxed you more and still spent more on new programs. The Republicans would have taxed you less and spent less. Neither of these solutions is the proper one: tax more and spend less. Therefore, politicians by definition are lousy budgeters.

But before I hear a chorus of "Throw the bums out!" go look in the mirror. You wouldn't elect a politician as dogcatcher if he campaigned on the platform of higher taxes and lower service. I have seen the enemy, and he is us.

The Federal Reserve is supposed to be above the mundane matters of governing. The Fed's job is simply to see what's right and go about doing it. Whether they are successful, I think, is beside the point. The responsibility clearly should be in their hands. When they have done it right, we have prospered mightily. Consider the period from Paul Volcker's time as chairman of the Fed to Alan Greenspan's terms. For the most part, these men got the tweaking of the money supply right, and the country prospered. That's not to be taken lightly, either. We have gone through some significant trauma over the last twenty-five years.

I shudder to think what might have happened if people of substance had not been running the Fed. If you want a taste of how bad it could be, think about the Great Depression, when the Fed got it completely wrong. At the precise time they should have been throwing open the bank vault doors, the Fed tightened credit, creating some of the most significant human misery in our history.

None of this discussion is designed to denigrate good fiscal policy. Tax cuts are important to a stagnant economy. Anything that takes money away from the bureaucracy and puts money into the hands of consumers benefits growth. The challenge for the individual investor is to be educated and experienced enough to see beyond the social significance of fiscal policy and examine its economic benefits in order to ascertain whether or not it is of macro significance, meaning it affects everyone, not just an individual.

Two schools of thought are involved in managing the nation's growth. One is mired in political point gathering (the government) and the other in academia (the Federal Reserve). Neither is reliable. Both are totally unpredictable. One may be preferable to the other, but even if the Fed does everything according to the book, the desired result might not be accomplished because this is not an exact science. In order to formulate any kind of economic forecast regarding the growth of the GDP, an investor needs to know both monetary policy (what the Fed's going to do) and fiscal policy (what the federal government's going to do).

The U.S. Dollar

When other countries buy our dollar as an investment, they do so because they believe our economy is better than theirs. The opposite is also true: they don't buy our currency as an investment when they think their economy is better. There you have it, all you need to know about the dollar. You can forget all of the mumbo jumbo: like when our dollar is weak, our exports are more attractive. That happens to be true, but it is not the salient point, given the dollar's value as an economic barometer.

Remember, the investor is trying to connect the dots: to glean the pertinent information from the economy in order to formulate an economic forecast that will cause him or her to either buy or sell stocks. Merely understanding what a fluctuating dollar does to the prices of goods and services is valuable but not necessarily conducive to making money in the American stock market.

Notice that I said the American stock market. The value of the dollar relative to other currencies can be instrumental in figuring out how much or how little foreign investment you ought to be considering. According to Jordan Goodman in *Everyone's Money Book*,

> While most of your assets will probably be in dollar denominated investments, you should be aware of the risk of currency movements if you own stocks or bonds denominated in other currencies. When you buy an individual stock or bond in another country, or a mutual fund that invests in foreign securities, the value of your investment fluctuates based on how many dollars it takes to buy a unit of the foreign currency. In effect, when you own a British stock, for example, your money has been converted into pounds. If the value of the pound falls against the U.S. dollar, your British shares will be worth less if you were to sell the stock and translate the pounds back into dollars. Conversely, if the pound gains value against the greenback, your British

stock will be worth more if you were to sell it. Currency movements, which swing day to day based on each country's economic and political conditions, can therefore hand you substantial gains or losses.[1]

Since asset allocation (proper diversification) is crucial to an investment portfolio's performance, understanding how the dollar is doing and forecasting how it will do is of paramount importance. Even if foreign assets represent just a tiny percentage of your portfolio (as they should), the impact can be profound, given the unlimited nature of the risk of owning foreign securities.

Remember, however, what we are trying to accomplish, and that should place the value of the dollar firmly into perspective. We are trying to determine how well or poorly the American economy is going to perform. It will help to have the opinion of the world community, and nowhere do you find that more perfectly than the dollar's stance against other currencies.

The Money Supply

An investor only needs a rudimentary knowledge of the business cycle and what makes us prosper or not decline. Whether you think that it's the Fed or the president, the Democrats or the Republicans, the gun lobby or the insurance guys, welfare or the Constitution, the economy is going to move in a fairly predictable pattern. In order to understand those patterns, you need to figure out where we are in the business cycle.

Here we are back to the Federal Reserve, which has a real role in affecting the direction of the money supply by lowering or raising interest rates. Raise rates and put less money in the system. Lower rates and put more money in the system. For all the reasons enumerated earlier, economies do better when money is loose than when it is tight.

The Economic Cycle

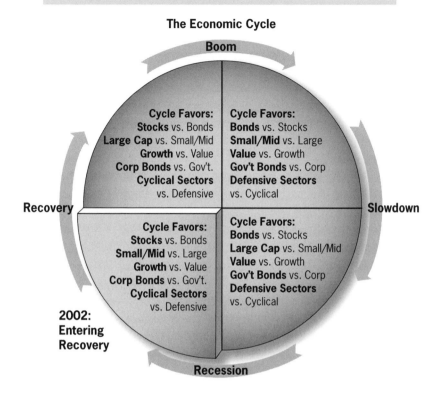

Boom

Recovery

Slowdown

Cycle Favors:
Stocks vs. Bonds
Large Cap vs. Small/Mid
Growth vs. Value
Corp Bonds vs. Gov't.
Cyclical Sectors vs. Defensive

Cycle Favors:
Bonds vs. Stocks
Small/Mid vs. Large
Value vs. Growth
Gov't Bonds vs. Corp
Defensive Sectors vs. Cyclical

Cycle Favors:
Stocks vs. Bonds
Small/Mid vs. Large
Growth vs. Value
Corp Bonds vs. Gov't.
Cyclical Sectors vs. Defensive

Cycle Favors:
Bonds vs. Stocks
Large Cap vs. Small/Mid
Value vs. Growth
Gov't Bonds vs. Corp
Defensive Sectors vs. Cyclical

**2002:
Entering
Recovery**

Recession

So understanding interest rates as a barometer for economic forecasting kills two birds with one stone.

Understanding whether the economy is expanding or contracting has a critical impact on one's money decisions. Where do you think we are right now in the economic cycle? Write your answer here: _____. Then test it against the information in the next chapter.

5

WHAT TIME IS IT?

The Journey from Fear to Greed

C an you remember learning to tell time? The excitement when you realized you knew how to read the hands on grandma's wall clock? The big hand and the little hand came together in a configuration that your brain could turn into information that you could use. "Eureka! So, that's what noon looks like!" Economic statistics are like that. They start out as just so much gobbledygook until you put the time and the effort into figuring out what the different patterns represent.

From there it's just a hop, skip, and a jump to figuring out the stock market's long-range direction based on the economic clock. When you think that it's six o'clock by the hands on the economic clock, that means that the stock market should do well, and when you think that it might be twelve o'clock, that means something entirely different for stock market performance. "Eureka! So, that's what a bull (good) or bear (bad) market looks like."

The Economic Clock

The first thing that we have to do is visualize the face of grandma's wall clock. At twelve o'clock, when the hands are pointing straight up, everything has been clicking economically. The stock market has been roaring, unemployment has been low, your job is stable. You feel good about life. At six o'clock, when the hands are pointing straight up and down, it's exactly the opposite. The economic news has been bleak, the stock market has been pretty lousy, you're worried about keeping your job, and you don't feel good about buying anything.

At twelve o'clock, write the word *GREED* in big letters. At six o'clock, write the word *FEAR*. At nine and at three o'clock, write the word *HOPE*. Are you starting to see a pattern here? We are applying the three emotions we talked about in chapter 4 to this graphic representation of our economic climate. Why? Because our economy is so influenced by them.

Let's look at some real-life examples of the effect these emotions have had on investors' economic decisions, which in turn impact the stock market.

Greed

In chapter 4, we saw how the business cycle is influenced by human fear and greed. That's talking about things in a macroeconomic sense (how the whole economy is influenced by the nation's collective fear and greed). Now, let's talk about how those same emotions when exercised by you (microeconomics) impact just you.

Greed is a sense that you are bulletproof. When you are comfortably in the grip of greed, advice becomes unnecessary. You know you can do no wrong. Greed can break you—believe me, I know. When I owned Shubooties, I thought I knew everything. After all, hadn't I made something from nothing? I had no doubt that I would be as big as Sears. I received counsel against what I was trying to do. I was told that it was too soon, that I was trying to grow the company too fast. I was told that I didn't have the experience or the cash flow. I was told all that, but I didn't hear any of it. Full speed ahead! That is the face of greed, and it is one ugly little puppy.

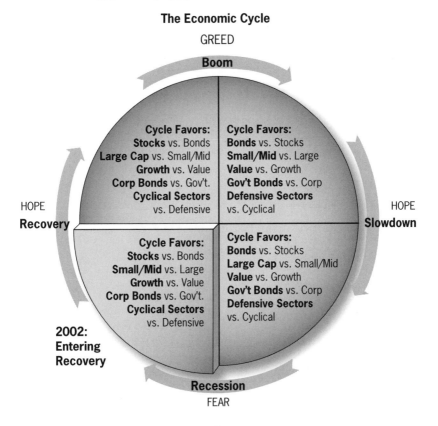

The Economic Cycle

GREED

Boom

Cycle Favors:
Stocks vs. Bonds
Large Cap vs. Small/Mid
Growth vs. Value
Corp Bonds vs. Gov't.
Cyclical Sectors vs. Defensive

Cycle Favors:
Bonds vs. Stocks
Small/Mid vs. Large
Value vs. Growth
Gov't Bonds vs. Corp
Defensive Sectors vs. Cyclical

HOPE
Recovery

HOPE
Slowdown

Cycle Favors:
Stocks vs. Bonds
Small/Mid vs. Large
Growth vs. Value
Corp Bonds vs. Gov't.
Cyclical Sectors vs. Defensive

Cycle Favors:
Bonds vs. Stocks
Large Cap vs. Small/Mid
Value vs. Growth
Gov't Bonds vs. Corp
Defensive Sectors vs. Cyclical

2002: Entering Recovery

Recession

FEAR

63

Greed is also the dominant emotion when the stock market is booming. Think back to the spring of 2000 when everybody and his brother believed they could make money trading stocks. The Super Bowl advertising list consisted primarily of Internet companies. The dot-commers had taken Wall Street by storm. Companies that had never made a nickel of profit went public, and their stock prices soared into the hundreds of dollars in a matter of days.

And all that led to greed, the kind that created stock day traders. One such gentleman called my radio show to tell me of his plans. "Danny," he said, "I want to know what you think because I respect your opinion. I recently quit my $200,000 a year job working for a pharmaceutical company. I quit to day-trade stocks on my computer. What do you think?"

"Let me ask you a couple of questions before I answer. . . . Are you married?"

"Yes."

"Do you have children?"

"Yes, two—a boy who's sixteen and a girl who's fourteen."

"Have you set aside money for their college education?"

"No."

"Do you have *any* money saved?"

"No, but I will save some."

"From what?" I asked.

"The money I make trading stocks."

"Didn't you have to put up some money before they let you trade?"

"Oh, yeah. I cashed in my 401(k)."

"Have you made any money yet?"

"On my first trade, I made $30,000."

"How have you done overall?" I asked. When the guy hesitated, I said, "Let me put it this way: how many trades a day do you make?"

"About fifty."

"What do they charge you per trade?"

"Eight dollars."

"Okay, so how are you doing to date?" I asked again, trying to get the guy to be accountable.

"Well, like I said, I went up thirty, and since then I've gone down fifty."

I could not believe what I was hearing. "So, net, you have lost $20,000. . . . Does that count what you pay for commissions on each trade?"

"No."

This guy had squandered $20,000 in trading losses at the same time that he paid the trading company about $32,000 in commissions. He'd lost a total of $52,000 *and* given up a lucrative job and sacrificed his kids' college educations. That, folks, is the face of greed. What's important to take from this conversation is that the guy was not alone.

When the market tanked, 60 *Minutes* profiled a couple of folks with stories very similar to this one. They were victims, they said. "The media and the trading companies made it sound so easy. I was lured into the abyss," was the common excuse.

Well, they may have been victimized. But it wasn't by the media or the stock market. The culprit in every case was greed.

Now, let's look at the six o'clock emotion, which also clouds rational investment: fear.

Fear

Fear is the most prevalent emotion in investment decisions. I'm talking about gut-wrenching, lose-all-your-money, become-a-ward-of-the-state, the-world-will-view-me-as-a-failure kind of fear. As with most emotions, perception becomes reality. In the case of fear, it becomes palpable; hence, prophetic. We cause to happen what we fear is going to happen.

In 1990 I was teaching my night school class on the basics of investing. One of my students, a gentleman about sixty years old, came to me for financial advice. He had heard me speak many, many times about the wisdom of buying quality stocks in a well-diversified portfolio and not panicking if something troublesome happened in the short term, especially in the first two years. He assured me that he had at least ten years before he would need the money, and he wanted it to grow. The man had $50,000 to invest, and we invested it in a diversified portfolio of well-known, dividend-paying, blue chip common stocks. This was in May of 1990.

At the end of that year, I got a phone call from this man, instructing me to sell all of his stocks, a portfolio that consisted of companies like Boeing, Merck, and Eli Lilly.

"Why would you want to do something like that?" I asked. "I know the portfolio is down some, but it represents quality. I thought you had ten years before even thinking about selling. Has that time frame changed?"

"No, the time is the same. It's just that my latest statement says that my $50,000 is now worth about $37,000. I can't afford that. Sell me out!"

"It's only worth $37,000 if you sell. You should not sell. If anything, you should think about buying more. Look, you are quitting a race less than one tenth of the way down the track. On top of that, you are riding the favorite. In fact, you are riding a horse that has never lost over this distance. Do not, I repeat, do not sell."

Well, I talked him out of that—for approximately two hours. He wouldn't give up his position, and since the $37,000 was his money, I sold him out. About three weeks later I was not surprised to receive transfer forms in the mail. No doubt he gave that money to whoever convinced him that I was wrong about not selling. I can tell you that I was not wrong.

Here's how I know. Four years later, while I was researching a commentary for television, the man's name popped up in my database. I wondered what the portfolio would be worth now. If this man had not sold, those very same stocks would have been worth $132,000 after four years. Instead, he lost $13,000 the day that he sold them (and lost $82,000 over the long run), and he did so for one reason and one reason only: he was afraid.

How does a reasonable, intelligent person make this kind of senseless mistake? That question has many answers, but I think it comes down to a lack of faith. I don't mean a spiritual kind of faith, although certainly a dose of that would have helped this situation immeasurably. No, I think this was a lack of faith in the economy. Or in the management of the companies. Or in the government. Or in the Federal Reserve. Or in research analysts. Any number of variables can force people into faulty decisions. But is it really any of those things?

I don't think so. Investors faced with an uncertain outcome ultimately have no faith in *themselves*. They know that they didn't do the work. In this man's case, he trusted me to do the work, but ultimately he didn't have faith that I knew what I was doing. His uncertainty created the lack of trust in me. Uncertainty breeds fear. Do you believe a car salesman if you know nothing about cars?

Throughout this book we will be looking at our finances through three different perspectives: the short term, the long term, and the eternal. An eternal perspective will help individual Christians to avoid responding to the business cycle with the emotions of fear and greed.

Think of the parable of the talents (Matt. 25:14–29). The three servants were each given an amount of money to invest for their master. The first tripled it, the second doubled it, and the third buried it in the backyard so he wouldn't lose it. The master's displeasure fell upon the third servant. The parable clearly illustrates that wasting one's abilities out of fear is displeasing to God.

The other side of the business cycle equation is no less displeasing to the Lord. Luke 12:15 tells us, "Watch out! Be on your guard against all kinds of greed; a man's life does not consist in the abundance of his possessions."

Isn't it interesting that these two variable emotions are so explicitly discussed in the Bible? Certainly that's understandable. The love of money can often displace our affection for the Lord. And that is a textbook definition of greed. References to money as the root of all evil aside, the Bible could not make it more obvious that human beings get into eternal trouble whenever they forget whose money they possess.

Let me close this discussion with a question. Do you believe that whenever you shuffle off this mortal coil, your entrance to paradise will be dependent upon the kind of car you drove?

Now that we have put an eternal perspective on the emotions that affect us, let's look at how these emotions—greed and fear—affect our economic climate.

Emotions and the Economic Cycle

Economically speaking, greed translates into boom, fear translates into bust, and hope translates into the hope that we are headed into a boom or not headed into a bust, depending on whether you think the clock is chiming nine (when the hands are going up to boom) or tolling three (when the hands are going down to bust). Think about this concept logically. In chapter 4 I told you about fear and how it translates into lower prices for growth vehicles like the stock market—and why that is precisely the time you want to be buying stocks. I also warned you that you wouldn't want to. At that point in the cycle, you are so scared of losing money, you can't conceive of trying to grow it. So here's the first huge concept about reading the economic tea leaves: when you think that it's six o'clock (those hands are straight up and down), buy stocks, and when you think it's twelve o'clock (those hands are up), sell stocks and capture the gains you should have made by owning those stocks as the economy moved from bust to boom. At twelve o'clock you need to move to a more defensive position.

Easy for you to say, Fontana, you think. *Who knows when it's six or twelve o'clock? Your fictional economic clock is not a precision instrument, like my watch.* True enough, but if you know the indicators and interpret them properly, most anybody can read the economic clock. I want to emphasize that merely knowing the indicators is not enough; you have to react to what the indicators are telling you. Most people can't do that since they are wrapped in either fear or greed. Fear won't let you buy, and greed won't let you sell when you should.

For the record, let me admit that this takes some talent. Controlling your emotions during periods of extreme financial stress is not easy. However, if you have the ability, you have a leg up on the competition. You simply have to maintain your composure, look at the economy tangibly, and evaluate it for what it is. In order to interpret the business cycle and accurately assess whether we are headed for boom or for bust, one needs a cool head.

Predicting the Economic Time

Let's take a closer look at the top and the bottom of the cycle. First of all, forecasting the stock market is an inexact science. You don't need the clock to hit six exactly before you buy stocks. Nor is it mandatory to sell at the stroke of twelve. It's perfectly fine to invest at four or five or seven or eight and sell at ten or eleven or one or two. You still made money. The point is that the cycle is an *indicator*.

The next thing investors need to remember is that the markets are predictive of future events. If you invest at five o'clock because you believe that the economic indicators point to better economic times ahead, remember that the recovery is going to take months to take effect. Therefore, you're going to have to allow time for the stock market to head north. It may even head south before heading north (especially if you invested at four or five). Your analysis was correct. You just need to be patient in order for your vision to play itself out.

Here's what the bottom of the cycle looks like economically. Remember our indicators? Interest rates, inflation, gross domestic product, the dollar, and the money supply. Six o'clock (bust) is when:

> interest rates are trending down
> inflation seems to be benign or falling
> the money supply is beginning to go up (this is a function of interest rates)
> gross domestic product is slowly (I repeat, slowly) rising
> the outlook for the dollar is strong

Remember, all of these indicators are positive, yet the clock will be pointing at bust. That is because the indicators predict *future* economic, and hence stock market, performance. You want to buy just after all the bad news is dissipating, before the general public realizes that we are headed into better times. This won't be all that tough since the media loves to tell you how bad the economy is long after it stops being bad.

On the other hand, twelve o'clock is when:

> interest rates are expected to rise
> inflation starts to creep back up
> the money supply goes down (again, a function of interest rates)

the rate of growth (GDP) starts to slow down

the dollar starts to lose strength

Remember, this is not an exact science. It will be enough to be reasonably accurate. But practically speaking, let's take a deeper look into an actual economic scenario and how it played itself out on the economic clock.

What time was it economically in July of 2003? Look at the economic data:

interest rates had declined twelve times

inflation was benign

GDP went up, emerging from recession in 2002

the dollar got strong before weakening

the money supply was way up (because interest rates were way down)

Except for a rather shaky dollar, we had a classic six o'clock scenario, and the stock market, as measured by the S&P 500 index, went up 25 percent for the year. Now, I need to remind you that the astute investor would have been adding stocks to his portfolio well in advance of July of 2003 in anticipation of the economic turnaround. After all, the Federal Reserve did lower interest rates twelve times. They did that over a period of years, not just in July of 2003.

That's the point. The astute investor would have been buying stocks when the normal investor, riddled with fear from the preceding recession, would have been selling. Obviously, from 1999 through 2002, more people were selling stocks than buying them. That's why the stock market declined for three years in a row. Would you have been anxious to buy stocks after they had just gone down for three years in a row? But that's what you should have been doing. And if you had been able to reason accurately that expansions follow contractions and that expansions are caused by lower interest rates, you would have been able to predict the economic recovery and gotten into the stock market at reduced prices.

We have seen that 2003 was a good example of six o'clock. Let's talk about 1999 to 2002 economically. Those four years were a great example of the top of the clock. First, let's look at the economy itself. I previously pointed out that economic expansions generally last for three or four years. The decade of the nineties produced the longest economic expansion in American history. That boom lasted an incredible nine years. Common sense alone would indicate that perhaps trees don't grow to the sky and maybe, just maybe, we were due for some form of contraction. But let's see if our indicators would have given us an even better idea of what lay ahead:

the Fed raised interest rates

the money supply declined as a result

GDP peaked at 7 percent (which was why the Fed raised the rates)

the dollar was very, very strong

inflation was benign but inching slowly upwards

Pretty close to twelve o'clock, don't you think? I need to interject a word of caution in all of this. I am not a proponent of market timing. I am not telling you that if you follow the business cycle, you will never encounter a stock market loss. I am trying to educate you about when you should accumulate stocks. You see, I don't think true wealth is accumulated by timing the stock market. True wealth is accumulated by buying stocks when the prices are cheapest and then selling them when your investment objective changes. That implies a buy-and-hold strategy over a long period of time.

The simplest strategy actually is to buy stocks when you start your working career, continue buying them for thirty or forty years, and then trim your holdings when you retire. If you do that, you will have accumulated Scrooge McDuck kind of money; I'm talking about throwing-it-up-in-the-air, filling-the-bathtub-with-coins kind of money. Donald Trump would never think of firing you!

A buy-and-hold strategy will accumulate wealth whether or not you have an MBA from Wharton or have ever read a single edition of the *Wall Street Journal*. Market timing per se is a colossal exercise in futility with a modest upside that's made less than modest by tremendous risk.

Unfortunately, most novice investors consistently think it's the bottom of the ninth with two outs, their team is trailing, and they are up to bat with two strikes on them. That's the perception. The reality, however, is that it's actually the top of the second with no score. Without the pressures of a time crunch, things look different, don't you think? Sure, they do. You have seven more innings before the game is over. That's a lesson most investors need to sear into their memories. Their stock market investments, provided they represent quality, will make them money. All investors need to do is manage their emotions when it looks like they are two runs down. The American business cycle is going to pinch hit for them, and it will be sending up Barry Bonds, Sammy Sosa, and A-Rod to boot.

Much of actual investment practice is based on what your Uncle Louie told you at a family gathering. Now, I'm certain that your Uncle Louie is a nice guy. I'm also pretty certain that your Uncle Louie, while he may have made a fortune on XYZ Corp., probably doesn't know squat about money and markets. I mean, honestly, have you ever met anybody who would admit to losing tens of thousands of dollars in the market? Ever? I haven't. Yet think about the years between 1999 and 2002. One would be hard pressed to find an investor who didn't lose tens of thousands of dollars in market value.

Men seem to be much, much worse about admitting this than women. Men, laden with testosterone, have a difficult time admitting they don't know much about handling money. Men believe they are supposed to know, as if they are born with the money gene implanted in their brains. However, we are all born completely ignorant of how to handle money. Think about it. We are not inherently blessed with the ability to balance a checkbook, manage credit card debt, apply for a mortgage, or make money investing in stocks. Yet men think it's in their DNA.

Women, no doubt wielding their considerable intellectual advantage, know they don't know much. Better yet, women know that men *think* they know, and women spend much of their married lives trying to get their husbands to realize that they don't know much without bruising their horribly fragile egos. Unfortunately, many times men are convinced that they are sadly equipped to manage money only after tens or even hundreds of thousands of dollars have suddenly disappeared from their brokerage statements or pension plans.

Therefore, both men and women need to admit to themselves the most basic of Wall Street axioms: *Nobody knows nothing!* Forgive the fractured grammar, but it's effective. "Nobody knows nothing" has been my maxim for over a decade of lecturing about finance.

If you ask a pseudo-expert what he thinks about today's market activity, he doesn't know the answer. But if he's on television, he'll pretend that he does. Why? Because if he doesn't, the media will never ask him for an opinion again.

This can also apply to radio and television anchors. Most of them have little financial background. They are journalists by vocation and investors by avocation. As one of the few financial professionals actively engaged in the mainstream media, I see this firsthand. (Now, I'm not talking about the folks on CNBC. Some of those folks do have financial backgrounds.)

Here's an example. Several years ago, I was preparing my commentary for the evening newscast when the telephone rang. I heard a male voice say, "You the money guy?"

"Yes, I am," I replied, even though I dislike being referred to as "the money guy."

"The market volume today was 500 million shares. Is that a lot, a little, or a ton?" The guy sounded young, and he was obviously inexperienced.

"It's a ton." (At the time, it was close to record volume.) "By the way, who is this?" I asked.

He told me his name and that he was the producer for a well-known network news program. "We're doing a story on the stock market, and I needed this information."

One incident like this sounds harmless enough, although I did find it odd that someone who sounded so young would be the producer of a network news show. Honestly, I didn't think much of it until the next day when the phone in the newsroom rang again.

The same voice from the day before said, "Is this the money guy?"

"Yeah," I answered as evenly as possible, even though some irritation was starting to creep into my voice.

"The market traded 550 million shares today. Is that a lot, a little, or a ton?"

I thought to myself, *Yesterday 500 million shares was a ton, and he needs to know if 550 million is a ton!*

"Nah, it's next to nothing. . . . They shouldn't have even bothered to open the doors." (Hey, the guy asked for it!)

Later that day I watched a very well-known television news anchor tell the nation that 550 million shares represented a slow day on Wall Street. While that is true today, ten years ago it was nonsense.

Unfortunately, that is how the news is gathered. It can be even worse at the local level. The local affiliates generally get their financial expertise from local bond or stockbrokers. The result is that the viewing and listening audience gets to hear what "the expert" wants them to hear. If the anchor interviews a bond guy, he'll make the case for bonds. If the reporter talks to a stock guy, most often he'll tell you to buy stocks. Duh.

The axiom "Nobody knows nothing" obviously refers to the short term. Wall Street experts do know about economies and investments over time. That's the point. The problem is that long-term predictions are just not dramatic, and certainly not sensational enough for television, radio, or newspapers that rely on ratings or subscriptions for revenues. Think about the contrast in these two headlines:

DOW GAINS 10,000 POINTS OVER LAST TWENTY YEARS
or
DOW PLUNGES 508 POINTS IN LARGEST SINGLE DAY LOSS IN HISTORY

Which headline do you think has more pizzazz? The answer is obvious. So why isn't the American public savvy to the manipulations of the American media? Sorry, I have no good answer to that question. But a few more questions might add some perspective: Why do we like to watch scary movies? How in the world is it possible for reality TV to be so popular? Not knowing why we aren't more intelligent consumers doesn't make the big ratings any less true. For whatever reason, we buy into the sensational. But you do not have to get caught in this media trap. You can tame your emotions.

By knowing—or at least having an educated guess— about the economic time, you improve your chances for investment success because knowledge settles the churning in your stomach that may or may not have been caused by a sensationalistic press.

This is not to say that the media doesn't have an important role to play in your research. It does, and it could be invaluable. But the principles of sound investing cannot be learned in front of a television, a newspaper, a magazine, or the pages of a book (even this one!). They can start there, but they most assuredly will not be honed there. You have to work your way through the financial quagmire, and experience is the best teacher.

Newspapers, magazines, television, and radio—these outlets cannot be beaten for information about economic indicators. However, they are also instrumental in whipping up investor frenzy. The headlines from the mainstream media will most often be dark. You will have to figure out when the public is buying into the fear or the greed fueled by the headlines. Hey, I never said you wouldn't need some talent. And, along with a healthy dose of talent, you also need to know how to manage risk by assessing your risk tolerance.

The individual investor hardly benefits from knowing what time it is economically—gauging the tea leaves correctly—if the result is still poor investment performance. What a shame that would be. Imagine having done all the work and made all the right conclusions only to destroy your chances for success by making the mistake of taking risks that you are not emotionally capable of handling, investing money that you don't have, or investing money that you are going to need in order to pay for an unforeseen emergency. Risk and the accurate interpretation of the various levels and types of risk is the subject of our next chapter. However, before we tackle that, let's try to put an eternal perspective on our investment motives. You can see that I don't advocate a short-term perspective on your investments. Long-term is much, much better. And that long-term perspective can be made even more accurate by seeing your investments through an eternal perspective.

The Eternal Perspective

Most of us think that getting rich is the be-all and end-all. I call this the "If Only Syndrome." If only I had a better job. If only I had a million dollars. If only I could win the lottery. If only_____(fill in the blank with your if-only) . . . then I truly could be happy. Most of these daydreams involve some kind of fantasy in which the daydreamers have a pile of cash poured on them through some kind of divine intervention or miracle. My mother, at age eighty, still believes that she is going to win the New York state lottery. I think most people harbor illusions just like that one. They are harmless enough until they become delusions.

Now, Wall Street is the master of delusion. Let me say this as plainly as I can: gambling is not investing. Gambling involves winning or losing very, very quickly. I don't think much good comes from trying to get rich quickly. After all, the gurus who tell you they know what is going to transpire in the stock market over the short run are at best disingenuous and at worst charlatans. So what's to be gained by listening and reacting to a guess?

We started this chapter gazing at your grandmother's clock. But we need to pay attention to another clock—an eternal clock. By keeping our eyes firmly on the big hand and little hand of God's clock, we can ascertain the season of our lives. Indeed, there is a season for everything, including the accumulation of wealth in order to serve those less fortunate than ourselves. The Almighty wants us to have life and have it abundantly. Part of the process of becoming a good steward over the Lord's possessions requires an accurate assessment of what we, as mortal human beings, can tolerate when we attempt to grow the Master's assets. That's next!

6

I Double Dog Dare You

Managing Risk

I think we all remember that childhood taunt, "I double dog dare you!" (For those of you who live north of the Mason-Dixon Line, that phrase might have been simply, "I double dare you.") Most of the time this chant was uttered after the suggestion of some feat of daring, some moment of sheer terror that could end up disastrously or wondrously depending on whether or not you managed to pull it off. Before deciding whether or not to chance it, you had to assess the risk.

I often think of those times when confronted with investment choices. Do I dare take the risk? Is the potential reward sufficient for me to risk my hard-earned dollars? And can I live with the results of an improper choice? Many times I have heard that inner voice saying, "Go ahead, Fontana. I double dog dare you."

In order to manage risk effectively, you need to know what risk is and what it is not. First, risk is not limited to the loss of money. Risk encompasses many different factors. Second, all risk can be mitigated by a return. And third, it is possible to lose money by not risking it.

In order to understand these three statements you need to be familiar with several different kinds of risk. Unfortunately, we tend to focus on just one: the likelihood that if we invest in something, we are going to lose our money. While I won't deny the pain associated with that particular outcome, you'll find it useful to know the other kinds of risk inherent in the investment world.

While there are many different kinds of risk, I am going to focus on the most common and the most basic risks for the individual investor. First, we will engage in a detailed discussion of purchasing power risk. You know it as inflation. Second, we'll talk about interest rate risk and the world of bonds. Next, we'll tackle business risk. We've got a bit of a leg up on that one since we discussed the business cycle in chapter 4. Then we will look at emotional risk and market risk, the risks of the markets themselves. Finally, I will show you how to minimize your risks through diversification. Ready? Here we go.

Purchasing Power Risk

How much did you pay for your first brand-new car? I paid $2,500 for a red 1965 Ford Mustang. Today, I don't think you can buy the four wire wheels for $2,500! That is purchasing power risk. You know it better as inflation, or the likelihood that goods are going to cost more tomorrow than they do today. Indeed, for the last fifty or sixty years inflation has averaged about 3 to 4 percent. On average that means that the cost of goods and services has gone up by that amount every year. If your investment returns do not average the inflation index after taxes at the very least, you are losing purchasing power. I call inflation "the midnight robber." It's a surreptitious thief.

In my office I keep a copy of the front page of the *New York Times* published on the day I was born. It cost $.03. Today that same paper would cost you $2.00 if you bought it in New York! That's sixty-six times more than it cost fifty-four years ago.

I remember my father saying when I was a teenager, "I fear the day is coming when you will walk into a grocery store with a bushel basket full of dollar bills and walk out with a loaf of bread." Well, a loaf of bread cost about nineteen cents at that time. My father wasn't far wrong.

Inflation is the enemy. You need to fight it with all your might.

Over the long haul (at least ten-year periods) common stocks have proven to be an effective hedge against inflation. In the eighty-eight years from 1900 to 1988, stocks (as measured by the Dow Jones Industrial Average) increased 2,855 percent while the cost of living (as measured by the Consumer Price Index) was up 1,162 percent. The numbers updated through 2003 are even more dramatic. However, during shorter periods of time, the inflation index has frequently outpaced stocks, and that gets investors nervous.

Look at the years from 1966 to 1974, from 1980 to 1992, and from 2000 to 2002. Or go way back in time and research the years from 1906 to 1914, from 1937 to 1942, and from 1946 to 1949. In each of these shorter periods of time, the stock market did not outpace inflation. However, the market has always recovered sufficiently to make up the difference and then some. From this historical analysis the investor should infer that purchasing power risk can be completely mitigated by time. Indeed, one can make the statement that there has never been a fifteen-year period when the stock market did not outpace inflation.[1]

If you compare the returns from common stocks, long-term corporate bonds, long-term U.S. government bonds, U.S. Treasury bills, and inflation, the most effective vehicle for outpacing inflation is common stock. According to the R. G. Ibbotson Associates in *The Stocks, Bonds, Bills, and Inflation Yearbook*, published in 1985, stock returns were positive in nearly two thirds of the years covered.[2] However, common stock is also much more volatile than the other types of investment.

The Ibbotson study of 1985 is fascinating on a couple of levels. The authors not only studied the past, they predicted the future. In their own words:

> The compounded inflation rate is expected to be 6.4% per year over the period 1976–2000 compared to the historical compounded inflation rate of only 2.3% over the period 1926–1975.
> The expected compounded return on common stocks for the period 1976–2000 is 13.0 percent per year. . . . Stocks are expected to have a compounded return of 6.3 percent after adjustment for inflation.[3]

They predicted that all the other investment vehicles would fare much worse. Let's see how close the authors got.

While inflation peaked at 13.3 percent in 1979, the 1980s saw a reversion to more moderate, though still substantial, inflation rates averaging about 5 percent. Inflation then continued to decline in the 1990s, down to an average 2.9 percent. The rate of inflation from 1976–2000 has averaged 4.17 percent. The Ibbotson Associates were off by 1.7 percent.

To put inflation into understandable terms, what cost $1.00 in 1926 would have cost $9.71 by the year 2000. If your investment plan doesn't take inflation into consideration, you risk not having enough money to maintain your present lifestyle.

Interest Rate Risk

Generally speaking, rising interest rates do not have a positive effect on stocks or bonds. When rates rise, volatility (those roller coaster swings that cause us perspiration) usually increases, and that's not good for an investor's psyche.

Let's suppose your Aunt Minnie wants to buy a house, and she makes a $90,000 offer on a cozy little bungalow because she can get a mortgage for a 4.25 percent interest rate. Aunt Minnie can only put down 5 percent on the loan. She's cutting it pretty tight since her monthly payments are going to be a little over $400, not counting private mortgage insurance (PMI), which she has to buy since she can't put down 20 percent or more for a down payment.

However, before Aunt Minnie can close on the house, the interest rate goes up to 4.5 percent, making the purchase much more challenging. Now she will have to come up with almost $450 each month (not counting PMI), and her income is only a thousand dollars, which makes her mortgage payment 45 percent of her income. As a result, Aunt Minnie decides to stay in her current apartment. The seller loses a buyer for his house, and the mortgage company loses a potential loan.

But that's not the entire effect of Aunt Minnie's decision. Rising interest rates can also affect the general economy. If Aunt Minnie had bought the house, she might have put even more money into the economy. For instance, she didn't like those red walls in the kitchen or the purple bedroom. Nor did she like the olive green carpet in the living room. She might have hurried to the store and bought new carpet and gallons of paint. And of course she needed some new furniture, since her apartment was smaller than the house. But Minnie didn't buy the house, so all those items didn't get purchased. The carpet company, the paint company, and the furniture company lost a customer. That year there will probably be quite a few Aunt Minnies out there, so she represents many lost purchases. Yes indeed, rising interest rates are not good for the housing market or for the general economy.

The same principle applies to the investment world. Suppose you purchase a bond paying a dividend of 4 percent, but a year or so later a new bond can be bought that will pay 5 percent interest. What do you think someone would pay you for your bond? Do you think it would be less than you paid? Of course it would. Why would anyone buy a 4 percent bond when they could have a 5 percent return from a new bond?

Certainly, the reverse is also true. If you own a bond paying a 5 percent dividend and the new bonds are paying 4, wouldn't people prefer to buy your bond? Of course they would. A bond investment may provide two ways for investors to make money. They get the interest rate (that's called the coupon), and they have the chance to sell the bond for more than they paid for it if interest rates decline and the bond becomes worth more than its face value (the capital gain).

Interest rates play a significant role in any investment portfolio because they affect the price of your investment vehicles. Higher interest rates make it more difficult for businesses to maintain sales and profits, and that impacts stock prices—and bond prices are negatively impacted as well. No, rising interest rates are not good for investments, while lower interest rates are most decidedly advantageous.

Lower rates mean that Aunt Minnie might be able to afford to buy that house and furnish, paint, and carpet it. That translates into higher stock prices for the mortgage company, the paint company, the carpet company, and the furniture company; their sales go up and, as a result, their profits go up. So let's sum up our discussion of interest rates this way: *up is bad, down is good.*

Business Risk

What happens to a business as a result of a downturn in the economy? Everybody needs clothing, but they may buy less in a difficult year. That's business risk.

We have already had a detailed discussion about the role of the Federal Reserve and the way the Reserve may or may not impact the business cycle. Keep interest rates low and you've got a shot at economic recovery. Raise the rates and "Houston, we could have a problem." As I mentioned, economists kick around different theories about the role of the Fed. Some think the Fed has too much power, so their discussion of business risk would center on the economy itself rather than the Fed's role in controlling it. For example, changes in the supply of raw materials or the invention of some new technology, such as robotics, could be responsible for changes in the business cycle.

While my thoughts might be somewhat revolutionary, I see some synergy between both theories. Clearly the Fed and what it does impacts the economy, and certainly Bill Gates and other innovators have had an enormous impact. For our purposes, we have to monitor both elements.

Emotional Risk

A financial advisor's job is to keep you from hurting yourself. Both fear and greed can tempt you to make investing mistakes you could easily avoid.

Switching Investments Due to Fear

Because of fear, most people want to *switch* their investments when they should hold them and vice versa. The risk in this scenario is you and your emotions. After experiencing significant losses in the stock market, many people switch to bonds. Then interest rates go up and their bond values go down. That, my friends, is getting whipsawed: killed in stocks and immediately thereafter killed in bonds, the classic double-dip. These losses from stocks to bonds mirror the boom (twelve o'clock) to bust (six o'clock) to boom (back to twelve o'clock) business cycle; such roller coaster swings make Ted Bundy look benevolent.

"But, Danny," you say, "look at the historical chart on pages 96 and 97. Bonds were only down two years out of twenty. That sounds pretty good to me." Well, if all you are trying to do is maintain your money, it's great. But if growth is your primary objective, bonds are not the answer (although they are an important buffer against volatility in appropriate allocations).

Look at all of the returns over the twenty years. A growth stock portfolio returns almost 11 percent per year compounded, doubling your money approximately every seven years. A bond portfolio returns half that, taking twice as long to double your money. Bonds, while safe, do not provide growth. They provide income and, depending upon the time you hold them, some potential stability.

What most investors do not realize is how much you can lose owning only bonds. In 1994, the Fed raised interest rates repeatedly and corporate bond investors lost a fourth of their money. How's that for safe? For every 1 percent rise in the federal funds rate, bond investors will lose approximately 12 percent of their investment. I can't tell you how many times I have informed clients that their bond portfolio has experienced some loss and they have exclaimed, "But they're bonds!" Sure are, and subject to risk like everything else. Don't let anyone double dog dare you to invest only in bonds.

Then, of course, you have the reinvestment risk to your income. Say you own bonds that pay 6 percent, and they mature. You get your money back; then you look to reinvest it and all you can find is 4 percent. On a $10,000 investment, you just lost $200 in income (the difference between $600 and $400). As you can see, if interest rates go up, your bonds lose value, and if rates go down, your income could go down when you look to reinvest. For a bond investor, the best scenario is a stable interest rate environment.

Those of you who just had your 6 percent certificate of deposit mature only to find that you can now only get 2 percent interest on a new CD know exactly the kind of pain I just mentioned. Having less income to apply to higher prices is a combination of two forms of risk: interest rate risk and inflation risk.

Let's pretend that you are retired and living off the interest generated from having $100,000 in a 6 percent CD that you bought ten years ago. The bank has been paying you $6,000 per year ($500 per month) for the last ten years. That money has been paying for your utilities, your phone, your cable television, and the insurance and gasoline for your car. When that certificate of deposit matures and you have to buy a new one, the bank only offers you 2 percent. That would only give you $2,000 a year—$4,000 less than they had been paying you. How would you make up the difference so you can pay those bills? Plus, do you think those bills would have remained the same over the last ten years? Chances are they've gone up.

But you can smooth out the potentially volatile risk scenario through proper asset allocation that includes stocks *and* bonds.

Yes, investors can be crippled by switching their investments because of their emotions—and they can also be harmed by that old emotion called greed.

Switching Investments Due to Greed

How many times have you heard a commercial on the radio touting this strategy or that technique which is guaranteed to turn hundreds of dollars into thousands of dollars? One particular pitch stands out in my experience. The guy used to advertise free seminars where you could learn to make $50,000 on one trade in the options market. As soon as I heard the commercial, I warned our radio station's general manager that this guy was a crook.

You cannot say what he was saying on the radio in the legitimate financial world. If I had said it, the National Association of Securities Dealers would have had my scalp. The only way this guy could get away with his claims was by not being regulated. There is no safe way to make $50,000 in the options market. So the guy was looking to make money from investors who, in all probability, would lose some of their money. In my mind that is the definition of a crook.

Radio, being radio, didn't care what the guy said as long as he paid for his commercial. So the station kept running the guy's ads. And I kept screaming about it on my show. I remember telling folks, "Stay away from that seminar in droves!" (I'm a lot of things, but wishy-washy is not one of them.)

A year later, the perpetrator was indicted. However, I promise you that he made a ton of money before that indictment. Furthermore, I predict that he shows up again someday soon, eager and able to scam even more people. You can easily see why somebody like that gets away with this junk. He's selling dreams fueled by investor greed. "Let me show you how to turn a buck into ten bucks in ten minutes with no risk" goes the pitch. And you know what? That's exactly what everyone wants to know. Unfortunately, P. T. Barnum was right: a sucker is born every minute.

Market Risk

Much has been written and broadcast about market risk. All one has to do is remember the performance of the stock market from 2000 through 2002 to understand what stock market risk can do to a portfolio. Much has also been written and said about managing current market risk by market timing. The allure of being in the market when it is going up and out of the market when it is going down is a powerful aphrodisiac. The simple fact that this is impossible to do consistently does not mute the allure. People want to feel they can do it. Some people actually believe they can.

Well, you can't! As much as you don't want to believe that simple maxim, you must. That core belief will save you tons of money, not to mention anguish. People may double dog dare you to consistently time the market. I warn you that the result may be disastrous. But take some solace in the fact that nobody else can do it either.

Long before I got into the investment business in 1985, Wall Street started anointing one financial guru after another. Joe Granville successfully predicted the rise in gold prices in the 1970s, so he was the hero *du jour*. After that all the rage was Bob Prechter and his Elliott Wave thesis, a system that forecast the market using an elaborate technical approach. Basically Prechter said that the market would move in waves, going from roughly 1,000 to 2,000, then back down to 1,300, and finally back up to 2,300 on the Dow Jones Industrial Average. Supposedly there were three waves. He was right on the first two. His last prediction proved to be unfortunate for investors—the last positive wave never materialized. Think about that. If someone had attempted to get into the stock market when the Elliott Wave said to, they would have experienced a quick and significant loss of principal triggered by the fear factor. The next guru was Elaine Garzarelli, who was widely credited with having predicted the stock market crash of 1987.

All of these gurus were very famous, some might even say notorious.

These Wall Street icons share a common thread: they all credit some kind of theory or system that will accurately predict stock movements over the short run. All are wrong, and their theories have been proven wrong. For example, Granville predicted that the stock market would be horrible in 1982. In fact, 1982 was the start of one of the longest bull markets in history. In the summer of 1996 Garzarelli forecast that the Dow Jones Industrial Average would fall to 4,000. In the winter of 1997, she reversed course when the Dow reached 7,000.

Let's add this axiom to our other tenets: *people who invest make money for themselves; people who speculate about the markets make money for their brokers.* That's why Wall Street hypes these kinds of strategies. If successfully predicting the market in the short run actually worked, wouldn't everyone be rich?

The elimination of market risk has to involve the elimination of a short holding period. Then an investment ceases to be speculation. Only by allowing enough time for an investment strategy to work itself out does an investor enhance the chance for profit. This is especially true for stock market investments. This obviously precludes the use of all short-term trading vehicles.

An investor doesn't invest in an Initial Public Offering (a new company going public for the first time) or a stock touted on the Internet. A *gambler* buys those. Investors buy stocks to hold for five, ten, fifteen, twenty, even fifty years.

Back in the mid-1990s, a penny stock firm used some fancy footwork to sell stock in a company called Treats International. For those who aren't aware, any stock under three dollars per share earns the dubious distinction of being called a penny stock. Its main attraction, I would imagine, is the opportunity that a penny stock presents an investor, and presumably, that's being able to "get in on the ground floor." What generally happens is that your money ends up under the ground floor.

As plainly as I can say it: Most of you need to stay out of the penny stock game.

Typically, penny stock firms will sell to anybody, including widows and orphans. I was stunned to hear that North Carolina investors bought over 500,000 shares of Treats International in the mid-1990s. That tells me that greed will sell a stock every time.

If someone calls you and offers you the opportunity to "get in on the ground floor," or if they guarantee you a return on your investment, hang up the phone—fast.

Better yet, ask for the prospectus on this fantastic, can't-miss deal and read it, cover to cover. Don't invest in penny stocks unless you can afford to lose your money, and I mean all of it. Buy a stock that has a good chance to be a good investment over the long haul.

This is not to say that an investor never, ever sells a stock. Buying and holding doesn't mean never selling a particular part of a portfolio. However, it does mean buying and holding a diverse portfolio of stocks across asset classes numbering in the hundreds, stocks which reflect the appropriate investment style and the appropriate weighting for each individual. That behavior alone mitigates market risk. The only way the average investor can own hundreds of stocks is through stock mutual funds. That's the only way your portfolio can be properly diversified.

By now you might be feeling overwhelmed by these five risks, which are only the most common ones. In fact, you might be saying, "I think I'll forget about investing in the stock market." But every investor needs to realize that in the world of investment, risk is pervasive. Such risk can be mitigated, but that process is complicated and must be carefully and scrupulously attended to. Let's look at some ways to minimize these risks.

Minimizing the Risks

The answer to minimizing risk is to assess your ability to tolerate the risk so you can position your assets accordingly. That's an easy proposition to discuss and a difficult one to carry out because of the gnawing ache in your stomach that comes from experiencing actual loss.

People seldom admit that they cannot tolerate losing their money. Most investors think of themselves as dashing desperados able to withstand all the slings and arrows anyone dares to toss their way. That's why I try to gauge people's ability to tolerate risk. I'm afraid my formula for this is not very scientific, but it does work. I simply ask people to imagine the following scenario.

Six months ago, your 401(k) statement showed a value of $10,000, and now it's only worth $9,000. On paper, it looks like $1,000 just disappeared. How does that make you feel?

When I present this to folks, I watch their eyes for a reaction. If I get just a slight twitch, I might ask them to imagine that instead of $9,000, the 401(k) is now only worth $8,000. Then I drop this amount even farther to $7,500. I keep going down until I get some movement that looks like an involuntary twitch response. It doesn't take very long for me to determine who can tolerate a 10 to 15 percent annual drop in the portfolio before they are ready to commit hari-kari. In this way, I can pretty much tell who can own stocks and how aggressively they can own them—and who should not invest in the stock market at all. This isn't foolproof, but it is useful. I will give you an opportunity to assess your own risk quotient at the end of this chapter.

Now let me give you a classic example of how not really understanding risk is the riskiest proposition of all. Let's say that your father acquired a large number of shares of stock from the company he worked for all his adult life. Let's pretend that it was the telephone company AT&T. Your dad dies and leaves the stock to you. At the time of his death, the stock is worth $500,000. It's all he had, and now it's all you have. Your entire invested net worth is tied up in one stock. Well, we all recognize the mistake: all your eggs are in AT&T's basket. Still, your rationale for not selling is that it served your dad well. "What was good enough for him is good enough for me," you say.

The example above is an actual case from my files of how a lack of diversification can kill an investor. One of my clients would not sell his American Telephone and Telegraph stock for love or money. He wouldn't even hear of it. Today what was once worth $500,000 is worth $19,600!

We all know that AT&T was one of the best blue chip companies throughout the latter half of the twentieth century—yet the company was not immune to poor management decisions. The result is the sad example outlined above. Folks, I don't care what company it is or how good you think it's going to be, allowing one stock to represent more than 2 to 3 percent of your total stock portfolio is subjecting yourself to massive risk.

Let's take this opportunity to talk about another mistake involving the same case example. Before the father died, he was advised to sell some of his AT&T stock in order to diversify his holdings. He was advised to sell at $500,000. He did not. When he died, the stock had plummeted and passed to the children at that value. He understood the logic but didn't want to sell because of the significant capital gains tax he would have to pay on his profit. The result was every bit as devastating as watching the stock price plummet. Here's the cardinal rule: *never do or not do something simply to save taxes.* If you have to pay a capital gain on your investment, guess what? *You made money!* That's not a bad thing. You can see how making a decision to save money ended up costing the investor a bunch more than he thought he might save.

In chapter 2, when I talked about the most common mistakes investors make, I spoke about the failure to diversify. However, assuming that you can solve the diversification issue by owning forty to fifty or more individual stocks is every bit as wrong as owning only one stock. *Diversification refers to ownership across asset classes: stocks, bonds, mutual funds, cash, real estate, and collectibles like gold coins or artwork.* Subcategories exist within each of those categories. For example, stocks can be growth stocks, value stocks, preferred income stocks, or utility stocks, to name a few, and those can then be further broken down into large, mid, and small capitalization stocks.

Let me give you some idea of the various styles of stocks that can be diversified. When my financial services team and I meet with a client, we show them a chart that analyzes the performance of various indices over the last twenty years. (See the chart on pages 96–97.) Included in the chart are:

Russell 1000 Growth Index (large cap growth stocks like Microsoft)

Russell 1000 Value (large, old, and well-known stocks like General Electric)

Russell 2000 Growth (small, new, and fast-growing stocks like Starbucks)

Russell 2000 Value (small and established companies)

MSCI EAFE Index (foreign companies in Europe, Asia, and the Far East)

Lehman Brothers Aggregate Bond Index (bonds)

Wilshire REIT (real estate)

The S&P 500 Index (an unmanaged portfolio of the 500 large cap stocks listed on all three major exchanges)

Notice the diversity inherent in those indices. You pretty much have all of the bases covered. Now, let's suppose that someone owns only large cap growth stocks (the Russell 1000 Growth Index) like Microsoft, Intel, and Cisco Systems. How would this person have done in the twenty years between 1982 and 2002? In its best year, the portfolio would have gone up 41.16 percent. Wow! Give me some of that, you say.

Yet in 2002 that same index went down 27.88 percent. Ouch! Over the entire twenty years, five years were down; one fourth of the time that portfolio lost money. But over the entire twenty years, *the portfolio increased on average 13.28 percent*. If Aunt Minnie invested $500 in the Russell 1000 Growth Index in 1982, she would have had over $6,000 by 2003.

Contrast that performance with the large cap value route exemplified by the Russell 1000 Value Index. The best year for that index showed a gain of 38.35 and the worst year a loss of 15.52 percent. *The average growth for that portfolio was 22.83 percent*. If Aunt Minnie invested her $500 in the Russell 1000 Value Index in 1982, she would have *over $30,000 by the end of 2003!*

Compare that to the small cap growth of the Russell 2000 Growth Index. That saw a high of 51.19 and a low of minus 30.26 percent. The average growth was 20.93 percent. If Aunt Minnie invested the $500 in the Russell 2000 Growth Index in 1982, she would have over $22,000 in 2003 when the market stabilized.

The international market as measured by the MSCI EAFE Index saw swings of up 9.44 percent in 1986 and a negative 23.45 in 1990. *The average growth was 12.57 percent*. If Aunt Minnie invested that $500 in the international market in 1982, she would have over $5,000 in 2003 when the market stabilized.

Bonds represented by the Lehman Brothers Aggregate Bond Index were the most stable performer over the entire twenty years, with only two negative years, a best performance of up 22.10 percent and a worst of down 2.92 percent. *The average growth was 10.02 percent*. If Aunt Minnie

1983	1984	1985	1986	1987	1988	1989	1990	1991	1992
Small Value 38.64%	Real Estate 21.89%	International 56.16%	International 69.44%	International 24.63%	Small Value 29.47%	Large Growth 35.92%	Bonds 8.96%	Small Growth 51.19%	Small Value 29.14%
Real Estate 32.17	Bonds 15.15	Large Growth 32.85	Large Value 19.98	Large Growth 5.31	International 28.27	S&P 500 31.69	Large Growth -0.26	Small Value 41.70	Real Estate 15.28
Large Value 28.29	Large Value 10.10	S&P 500 31.73	Real Estate 19.74	S&P 500 5.25	Large Value 23.16	Large Value 25.19	S&P 500 -3.11	Large Growth 41.16	Large Value 13.81
International 23.69	International 7.38	Large Value 31.51	S&P 500 18.67	Bonds 2.75	Small Growth 20.37	Small Growth 20.17	Large Value -8.08	S&P 500 30.47	Small Growth 7.77
S&P 500 22.56	S&P 500 6.27	Small Value 31.01	Large Growth 15.36	Large Value 0.50	Real Estate 17.48	Bonds 14.53	Small Growth -17.41	Large Value 24.61	S&P 500 7.62
Small Growth 20.13	Small Value 2.27	Small Growth 30.97	Bonds 15.27	Real Estate -6.59	S&P 500 16.61	Small Value 12.43	Small Value -21.77	Real Estate 23.84	Bonds 7.40
Large Growth 15.98	Large Growth -0.95	Bonds 22.10	Small Value 7.41	Small Value -7.11	Large Growth 11.27	International 10.54	Real Estate -23.44	Bonds 16.00	Large Growth 4.97
Bonds 8.36	Small Growth -15.83	Real Estate 7.02	Small Growth 3.58	Small Growth -10.48	Bonds 7.89	Real Estate 2.72	International -23.45	International 12.13	International -12.17

■ Large-Cap Growth = Russell 1000 Growth Index □ International = MSCI EAFE Index
■ Large-Cap Value = Russell 1000 Value Index ■ Bonds = Lehman Brothers Aggregate Bond Index
■ Small-Cap Growth = Russell 2000 Growth Index □ Real Estate = Wilshire Reit Index
■ Small-Cap Value = Russell 2000 Value Index □ S&P 500 Index

invested her $500 in the Lehman Brothers Aggregate Bond Index in 1982, she would have $3,376 in 2003.

Real estate had its best year in 1996, increasing 37.04 percent, while 2002 saw it decline 22.09 percent. The average growth was 11.24 percent. If Aunt Minnie invested that $500 in real estate in 1982, she would have over $4,200 when the market stabilized in 2003.

The S&P 500 Index was up 37.58 percent for its best performance and down 22.09 for its worst. The average growth was 13.98 percent. If Aunt Minnie invested that

1993	1994	1995	1996	1997	1998	1999	2000	2001	2002
International 32.56%	International 7.78%	Large Value 38.35%	Real Estate 37.04%	Large Value 35.20%	Large Growth 38.70%	Small Growth 43.10%	Real Estate 31.04%	Small Value 14.02%	Bonds 10.27%
Small Value 23.84	Large Growth 2.66	S&P 500 37.58	Large Growth 23.12	S&P 500 33.36	S&P 500 28.57	Large Growth 33.14	Small Value 22.81	Real Estate 12.36	Real Estate 3.60
Large Value 18.12	Real Estate 2.66	Large Growth 37.19	S&P 500 22.96	Small Value 31.69	International 20.00	International 26.96	Bonds 11.63	Bonds 8.42	Small Value -11.43
Real Estate 15.46	S&P 500 1.32	Small Growth 31.04	Large Value 21.64	Large Growth 30.49	Large Value 15.63	S&P 500 21.05	Large Value 7.04	Large Value -5.59	Large Value -15.52
Small Growth 13.36	Small Value -1.55	Small Value 25.75	Small Value 21.37	Real Estate 19.67	Bonds 8.68	Large Value 7.35	S&P 500 -9.11	Small Growth -9.23	International -15.94
S&P 500 10.08	Large Value -1.99	Bonds 18.47	Small Growth 11.26	Small Growth 12.95	Small Growth 1.23	Bonds -0.83	International -14.17	S&P 500 -11.87	S&P 500 -22.09
Bonds 9.75	Small Growth -2.43	Real Estate 12.24	International 6.05	Bonds 9.66	Small Value -6.45	Small Value -1.49	Large Growth -22.43	Large Growth -20.42	Large Growth -27.88
Large Growth 2.90	Bonds -2.92	International 11.21	Bonds 3.63	International 1.78	Real Estate -17.00	Real Estate -2.57	Small Growth -22.44	International -21.44	Small Growth -30.26

$500 in the S&P 500 Index in 1982, she would have over $6,800 when the market stabilized in 2003.

Now, everyone would like to believe that they have the talent to buy those indices in their best performance years and to avoid them during their worst. Again, it's tempting double dog dare to do so. The truth is that most of us buy the best performers long after they have performed at their best, typically after Uncle Louie told us how well he did buying that particular asset class. We rush out to buy it too. The truth is, we are probably buying what Uncle Louie is selling.

So how can the average investor mitigate his or her own emotions when the market either craters or explodes skyward?

You buy them all! That's true diversification. Does it work? Well, let's see. Let's look at the same chart with an eye on the diversified portfolio's performance.

For our purposes, we are going to buy 20 percent each of large growth stocks, large value stocks, and bonds. We are then going to complement that portfolio with an additional 10 percent each of international stocks, real estate, small cap growth stocks, and small cap value stocks. Here's what that diversification looks like:

Large Cap Growth	20%
Large Cap Value	20%
Bonds	20%
International Stock	10%
Small Cap Growth	10%
Small Cap Value	10%
Real Estate	10%
Total	100%

How would we have done with that investment profile? Pretty darn good! Our best year would have been 1985, with an increase of 32.33 percent, while our worst year would have been a decline of 11.54 percent in 2002. *The average growth would have been 12.17 percent.* If Aunt Minnie had diversified her $500 of holdings in this way, she would have had *almost $5,000 when the market stabilized in 2003.* Now, I will admit that Aunt Minnie could have done better if she had invested only in the Russell 1000 Growth Index (over $6,000), the Russell 100 Value Index (over $30,000), the Russell 2000 Growth Index (over $22,000), the S&P 500 Index (over $6,800), or even the MSCI EAFE (over $5,000). But that breaks all the rules of diversification and asset allocation.

Take the Russell 1000, for instance. Even though you might have made over $6,000 by 2003, between 1982 and 1983 you would have lost 40 percent of your money. How many of us can stomach a 40 percent loss? Imagine that it's a million dollars and that in one year you lose $400,000. Even if you're not talking about a million-dollar investment, the impact of your investment on your life can be just as threatening, because in one year you are significantly destroying that which has taken you decades to accumulate. If Aunt Minnie had all her money in the Russell 1000, she probably would have pulled her money out when she saw those losses and thus missed out on the long-term profitability.

The method to this madness has another sublime benefit: the ride is so much smoother, and a smooth ride keeps fear in check. Aunt Minnie has avoided a heart attack or a stroke by not worrying over big swings in one market.

I think it's safe to assume that most people would not be overcome with fear if their portfolio only went down by 11 percent in any given year. They wouldn't like it, but they wouldn't panic. Declines of 25 to 30 percent or more cause panic and inappropriate behavior. Eleven percent might cause some consternation, but I actually think that an 11 percent decline in 2002 when the S&P 500 Index declined 22.09 percent might have caused you to feel a sense of pride at how smart you were against the field.

Remember one really important point in all of this: *diversification does not protect you against loss.* The stock market does not come with guarantees. However, *diversification does cushion volatility.* The issue becomes personal, however. How much volatility can each individual bear? Put another way, how much reward can one reasonably expect? We all want the thrill of quick money. It makes blood course faster through our veins. On the other hand none of us enjoys the consternation of watching the experiment failing miserably.

With that in mind, take a moment to evaluate your risk quotient.

Risk Analysis

1. Your age is
    _____ under 30.
    _____ 30–40.
    _____ 41–50.
    _____ 51–64.
    _____ 65 or over.
2. You have saved for a big vacation. Two weeks before your departure, you lose your job. You
    _____ cancel your vacation.
    _____ make plans for a modest vacation at the beach instead.
    _____ go as scheduled, reasoning that job hunting will go better after a good vacation.
    _____ extend your vacation and plan a real blowout; this might be your last opportunity to go first class.
3. Your current income is
    _____ under $25,000.
    _____ between $25,000 and $50,000.
    _____ between $50,000 and $100,000.
    _____ over $100,000.
4. You are financially responsible for
    _____ only yourself.
    _____ older parents.
    _____ both children and spouse.
    _____ bills split with working spouse, no kids.
    _____ bills split with working spouse and kids that you both support.
5. Your job
    _____ is iffy.
    _____ is secure with good potential for income growth.

_____ doesn't matter because you expect a large inheritance.

_____ doesn't matter because you expect to go out on your own soon.

6. After you make an investment, you typically feel
   _____ thrilled.
   _____ satisfied.
   _____ confused.
   _____ regretful.

7. You take a job at a fast-growing company, where you are offered these choices. You pick
   _____ a five-year employment contract.
   _____ a $25,000 bonus.
   _____ a 10 percent pay increase on your $100,000 salary.
   _____ stock options (the opportunity to buy company stock at a set price) with a current value of $25,000 but the chance for appreciation.

8. This statement best describes you
   _____ I don't see any point in saving.
   _____ I'd like to save something, but there's never anything left over.
   _____ I try to save a little whenever I can.
   _____ I save 5 percent or more of my salary, regardless of other circumstances.

9. You invest $10,000 in a stock that drops 10 percent in value the following day. You
   _____ put in another $10,000 while it's down.
   _____ sit tight because you did the research.
   _____ sell and go back to certificates of deposit.
   _____ wait for the stock to regain the $1,000 loss, then sell it.

10. Describe your investment knowledge. Choose one.

_____ I am a knowledgeable investor who's able to explain concepts such as standard deviation and risk measurements.

_____ I understand how mutual funds work and feel confident discussing the best funds in different categories.

_____ I have only a vague idea about financial terminology.

_____ I never get into financial discussions because I don't understand any of the concepts.

11. How would your spouse or best friend describe you as a risk-taker?

_____ foolhardy

_____ willing to take risks after research

_____ cautious

_____ risk averse

_____ afraid of your own shadow

12. How would you describe yourself as a consumer of investment information?

_____ I am a business news junkie, spending hours a day digesting investment information.

_____ I regularly read the *Wall Street Journal* and at least one specialized business publication.

_____ I spend about twenty minutes a day on the financial pages.

_____ I watch the business news on television but don't understand much.

_____ I avoid business news whenever possible.

13. How far away are your major financial goals?

_____ less than two years

_____ two to five years

_____ five to ten years

_____ more than ten years

14. When you are faced with a major financial decision, you
    _____ flip a coin.
    _____ agonize.
    _____ call each of your friends and ask what they would do.
    _____ go with your gut.
    _____ research the options.

15. How do you feel when you suffer a financial loss?
    _____ I think I'm a bad person.
    _____ I feel guilty.
    _____ I view it as a personal failure.
    _____ I see it as an obstacle to be overcome.
    _____ I almost never suffer losses, because I don't take risks that would lose me money.

16. Your employer offers a year's severance pay to the first 100 employees who accept the offer. You
    _____ take it immediately.
    _____ take it only if you had been researching business opportunities and felt you had a good option ready to go.
    _____ start looking; you can't afford to leave now, but you're not going to wait for the other shoe to drop.
    _____ ignore it; you intend to spend the rest of your career with this company.

17. You invest in emerging markets, believing they will grow over the next decade. Soon they are down 20 percent. You
    _____ sell.
    _____ double your holdings.
    _____ do nothing.

_____ wait until the end of the year to rebalance, adding to your stake if necessary to bring it back to 10 percent.

18. Your savings—including retirement plans—are
_____ nonexistent.
_____ embryonic.
_____ equal to six months' salary or less.
_____ equal to one year's salary.
_____ equal to two years' salary or more.

19. Which best describes you?
_____ living with parents
_____ apartment with roommates
_____ own a starter home
_____ saving to trade up to your dream home
_____ ensconced in the home of your dreams—or close enough that you're prepared to stay

20. How would you describe your overall income status?
_____ I survive paycheck to paycheck.
_____ I have a small amount of savings.
_____ I have an income of more than $50,000 and a modest portfolio of investments.
_____ I have substantial holdings that include an investment portfolio of investments, savings, insurance, and retirement accounts.

This may have given you an idea of your own risk tolerance, but my suggestion is that you take your questionnaire to a professional financial advisor and have him or her evaluate it. A professional can help you evaluate your willingness to take risks *and* help you minimize risks wisely.

7

THE KNEE BONE'S CONNECTED TO THE SHIN BONE

Asset Allocation

Probably no phrase is more misunderstood and overused in the financial world today than *asset allocation*. These two words are truly the buzzwords of the new millennium. But what do they mean? Furthermore, even if you understand asset allocation, will you employ it? I'm certain that asset allocation is the most necessary tool for dampening the volatility in an investment portfolio.

In the last chapter you learned to take your risk temperature by consulting a financial advisor. In this chapter I am going to attempt to show you how to apply your level of risk to the appropriate percentage of investment assets.

Understanding Asset Allocation

Asset allocation is different from diversification. Diversification implies that you need to own different types of investment assets, divided between stocks, bonds, real estate, and cash. *Asset allocation tells you how much of each you need to own, given your present investment circumstances.* Asset allocation gets to the heart of risk management.

Most people pretty easily understand that an investor should own different types of investments. That concept is best described by the age-old axiom "Never put all your eggs in one basket." But in my career as a financial advisor, I see too many examples of investors ignoring proper asset allocation. Instead they take the easy way out: they apply equal investment percentages to asset classes.

For example, an investor will pick five different types of investments and invest 20 percent in each, thinking he has all the bases covered. This is the classic asset allocation mistake. Instead, investment percentages should be determined from the investor's profile. Who is he? Is his job stable? How old is he? Does he have any debt? The list of questions is extensive, and we have covered them already. Individuals need to have their portfolios customized to their circumstances.

What I am describing is a particularly modern phenomenon. In the old days, investors used to try to find investments that were undervalued in order to sell them later at a profit, one at a time. Today we see assets as a component of a portfolio—cogs in a wheel, if you will. Each asset has a job to do so the wheel can turn effectively. Each asset, chosen in a *precise* percentage, is expected to complement the others. I could show you a fancy chart that measures risk on different asset classes, but I don't think you need to know the technical stuff. Just grasp that different investments react differently to economic conditions.

Another way to think of it is as a recipe that has no equal parts. For instance, here's the recipe for the Fontana Growth Soufflé:

Fontana Growth Soufflé
Serves: A twenty- to thirty-year-old investor with thirty or more years left to work.

Ingredients: large cap growth stocks; mid cap growth stocks; small cap growth stocks; large cap value stocks; mid cap value stocks; small cap value stocks; international large, mid, and small cap stocks; bonds; real estate; and cash.

Directions:
    Reserve 4 percent of your total assets for cash.
    Invest 23 percent of your assets in large cap growth stocks.
    Invest 14 percent of your assets in mid cap growth stocks.
    Invest 8 percent of your assets in small cap growth stocks.
    Invest 15 percent of your assets in large cap value stocks.
    Invest 10 percent of your assets in mid cap value stocks.
    Invest 5 percent of your assets in small cap value stocks.
    Invest 5 percent of your assets in large cap international growth.
    Invest 5 percent of your assets in mid cap international growth.
    Invest 5 percent of your assets in small cap international value.
    Invest 3 percent of your assets in government bonds.
    Invest 3 percent of your assets in real estate securities.

Mix together. Start cooking immediately and maintain for the appropriate period of time or to taste (in other words, until you attain your goals).

107

Note that this recipe is for a "Growth Soufflé." And the recipe only serves a twenty- to thirty-year-old investor. (If this isn't your profile, don't worry. I will give other recipes that are appropriate for other investors later in the chapter.) The recipe would be different to serve different investors, and the recipe would further vary by the amount of time individuals have to let their assets "cook." The important thing to remember is that there are as many recipes as there are individuals.

Everyone has different likes and dislikes. For instance, many of us are allergic to some particular food, or at the very least don't like it. The successful chef leaves those elements out of a guest's dinner. Much as my wife, Mary, might ask our dinner guests prior to their arrival, "Are there any foods you can't tolerate?" I might ask an investor, "Are there any risks you just can't stomach? Any particular types of investment that you just won't make?" It is then up to me, based on their answers, to design the soufflé most palatable to them, just as it's up to Mary to eliminate the shrimp cocktail if a guest is allergic to seafood.

At the same time, investors need to recognize their lot in life. A sixty-year-old should not consider the same percentage ingredients as a thirty-year-old. It's important to note that the ingredients might be the same; the difference lies in the amount used in the recipe. A thirty-year-old might be willing to slather on the hot sauce, while a sixty-year-old would use just a trace for flavor. Investors really need to be aware of their shortcomings in this area. I would strongly urge you to ask for advice rather than attempt to do this on your own.

I also have a bone to pick with the financial services industry in this matter. I am certain that you have all seen the boilerplate investment portfolios typical in mutual fund marketing materials. They will suggest a couple of asset allocations that will generally be very, very broad. They might describe the allocations as "aggressive, moderate, and conservative."

My problem with this approach is that it does not go far enough. Your idea of aggressive and my idea of aggressive most likely differ. I can tell you from experience that most novice investors like being labeled "aggressive," even though they are actually quite conservative when it comes to loss. The problem is, they won't know this until they take the aggressive allocation, see their portfolio decline, and then react emotionally and sell at the wrong time, resulting in a loss. That's why this has to be a hand-holding exercise, and you are best served sitting across the desk from a financial counselor. While this is no guarantee of a mistake-free exchange, you do minimize the likelihood of making an egregious mistake.

One might wonder why all the hoopla over asset allocation. I mean, after all, can't an investor do well by buying and holding quality stocks over a long period of time? While the answer to that question might be yes, it could also very easily be no. I don't like the odds. That's precisely the point. Asset allocation puts the odds in your favor.

Here's what I mean. Over the years and with the advent of computer technology, the financial services industry has been able to predict future success with some measure of accuracy by plugging gobs of investment scenarios into computers. This process is called the Monte Carlo Method, and I have used it extensively in my practice.

Under this process, we plug in a client's mix of investments and factor in some demographic information. Do the clients consider themselves conservative, moderate, or aggressive in their approach to investing? How old are they? Do they need income? A whole host of questions get plugged into the computer dynamic. The results are a projection of the likelihood that the investors, given their individual profiles, will reach their objectives.

If the clients end up with at least a 75 percent chance of reaching their goals, I consider the exercise comfortable. If the profile comes back with a 90 percent chance of success, I might think they are being too aggressive. If it's less than a 60 percent chance, I might think they are being too conservative. The point is that this method is different from the quick Fontana Growth Soufflé I mentioned earlier in this chapter. This is a scientific approach to a very difficult task.

Let's look at a few Fontana soufflés for different investment profiles, just to give you an idea of what I mean. But remember, these are boilerplate profiles, not specific portfolios designed for particular individuals. I only give them to you here to suggest the type of portfolio you might consider. You can begin your thinking here, but if you really want to reduce your risk, you need to consult a professional who can design a specific portfolio for you.

Profiles of Asset Allocations

Try to identify yourself in the following descriptions. The ingredients are the same for each profile, but the percentages of individual asset allocations are very different.

Low Risk

Low-risk investors seek some increase in the value of their investments while maintaining a high level of protection for their money. They require more income than growth but are willing to sacrifice some income in pursuit of safety. These people have a moderate time frame, about ten to twenty years. Though risk avoidance is a primary objective, this strategy seeks to enhance performance through exposure to both large and mid capitalization equity investments by placing the majority of portfolio assets in bonds rather than cash.

The Fontana Soufflé for the Low-Risk Investor
Ingredients: cash; intermediate (five- to fifteen-year maturity) taxable bonds; large cap equity; mid cap equity; small cap equity; and international equity.

Directions:
>   Reserve 20 percent of your assets for cash.
>   Invest 55 percent of your assets in taxable bonds.
>   Invest 10 percent in large cap equities.
>   Invest 5 percent in mid cap equities.
>   Invest 10 percent in international equities.

Mix together. Start cooking after retirement and maintain for the rest of your lifetime.

Conservative Growth

Conservative growth investors have two objectives: capital appreciation and current income. These people also have a moderate time frame, perhaps fifteen to twenty-five years, and seek the potential for appreciation at the same time that they control risk. The recipe would call for mostly fixed income investments and equities that are widely diversified.

The Fontana Soufflé for Conservative Growth
Directions:
>   Reserve 6 percent of your assets for cash.
>   Invest 50 percent in intermediate taxable bonds.
>   Invest 15 percent divided between large cap growth stocks and large cap value stocks.
>   Invest 9 percent, divided between mid cap growth stocks and mid cap value stocks.
>   Invest 5 percent, divided between small cap growth stocks and small cap value stocks.
>   Invest 15 percent in international equities (large cap, mid cap, and small cap).

Start cooking three to five years before retirement and continue cooking until well after retirement or until your health declines. Then switch to the low risk recipe.

Moderate Growth

Moderate growth investors try to grow their money with a secondary goal of current income. These investors can stomach some reasonable swing in the value of their portfolio over a medium- to long-term horizon (10–20 years) in order to get where they need to go. This strategy tries to provide growth through equity exposure, properly and widely diversified, while relying on some fixed income both to lower the risk and to add some minimal income to their mix.

The Fontana Soufflé for Moderate Growth

Directions:

Reserve 1 percent of your assets for cash.

Invest 30 percent in intermediate taxable bonds.

Invest 25 percent in large cap stocks, divided between growth and value.

Invest 14 percent in mid cap stocks, divided between growth and value.

Invest 10 percent in small cap stocks, divided between growth and value.

Invest 20 percent in international equities (mixture of large, mid, and small cap).

Start cooking around age fifty and hold until just before retirement, when you should consider switching to a conservative growth profile.

Long-Term Growth

This is the meat and potatoes of all the Fontana recipes. Long-term growth investors have growth as their primary investment objective. They will have a moderate- to long-term time frame (at least twenty to thirty or even forty years) and a very low need for income. The long time frame allows them to ignore stock market price fluctuations, since they will live through several business cycles. This strategy is designed to offer considerable appreciation within known risks.

The Fontana Soufflé for Long-Term Growth

Directions:

Reserve 1 percent for cash.

Invest 45 percent in large cap stocks, divided between growth and value.

Invest 15 percent in mid cap stocks, divided between growth and value.

Invest 14 percent in small cap stocks, divided between growth and value.

Invest 25 percent in international equities (mixture of large, mid, and small cap).

Mix and hold for a very, very long time. Start young and finish old.

Notice there are no bond investments in this soufflé. This recipe is also more specific than the Fontana Growth Soufflé I suggested at the beginning of this chapter.

Aggressive Growth

Aggressive growth investors are trying to make the most money they possibly can. They have zero need for income. They can tolerate swings in the market in exchange for the long-term reward. This is a high-risk portfolio because of its emphasis on the small to mid cap market. Returns in this recipe are often higher than the other recipes, but these areas also offer the highest risk. Again, notice that this soufflé has no bond allocation.

The Fontana Soufflé for Aggressive Growth

Directions:

Reserve 1 percent for cash.

Invest 14 percent in large cap stocks, divided between growth and value.

Invest 15 percent in mid cap stocks, divided between growth and value.

Invest 45 percent in small cap stocks, divided between growth and value.

Invest 25 percent in international equities (mixture of large, mid, and small cap).

Mix and hold for a very, very long time. Start at the beginning of your career and finish at the very end.

By now I hope you realize that everybody is different. The recipes above should not be followed to the letter but should be adapted to your individual circumstances. However, they do give you some idea of what your portfolio should look like at particular times in your lifetime. This is about exercising some discretionary thinking about your individual circumstances and how that affects the positioning of your investment assets at crucial moments in your lifetime.

Have you ever started an exercise program after a lengthy period of a sedentary lifestyle? Did you perhaps try to do too much, forgetting that you are fifty years old instead of twenty? That's kind of what happens when you don't take into account your investment muscle memory. The first day feels okay, but the next day every bone in your body aches. Let that be the lesson. Act your age in your investment portfolio.

8

THE HEART OF THE MATTER

Managing Your Emotions

Too many times in my financial management career people have assured me of their ability to handle the downside of markets, only to disappoint me and destroy their investment program as a result of that inability. By now you know the significance of fear, hope, and greed in an investment portfolio's performance. By now you know the do's and don'ts of portfolio construction. You know how to read the economy, diversify a portfolio for optimal performance, and limit risk through asset allocation. You have all the technical tools. What you may or may not have is the courage to make it work. Let's look back at two emotions—fear and greed—to make sure you truly are able to handle the downside of the market.

Antidotes to Fear

Chicken Little warned us, "The sky is falling!" That fictional character had nothing on the financial press. So many times over my twenty years in the investment business, I have heard both commentators and ordinary individuals refer to the economy by saying, "It's never been this bad." You heard this trumpeted repeatedly through the financial press in the years 2000 to 2004. Do the following statements sound familiar? The trade deficit is too high. The unemployment number is not low enough. Productivity is not where it needs to be. The war in Iraq is a mistake. George W. Bush could have prevented the attacks of September 11, 2001. The list is a long one, designed to have you believe that "It's never been this bad."

My advice about long-term investing is meaningless if the investor cannot get past short-term fear. Here's the answer: not only is the sky falling but it has fallen many times before. And that's the secret. It *has* been this bad throughout our history.

Let's look at seventy-five years of the way the economy has fluctuated during perilous years of American history, and you tell me if it has ever been this bad before. Ready? Here we go.

1929	The Great Depression (26 percent unemployment)
1939	World War II
1945	The atomic bomb dropped
1950	The Korean War begins
1963	President John F. Kennedy assassinated
1964	Vietnam War
1973	Arab oil embargo (recession begins)
1974	Watergate scandal; President Nixon resigns (recession continues)
1978	22 percent prime interest rates, 15 percent inflation under President Carter
1979	Iran hostage crisis

1981	President Reagan shot (recession of 1981–1982)
1987	Stock market crash: market falls 40 percent in three months
1990	Persian Gulf War
1994	Weak dollar
1997	President Clinton impeached
2001	Terrorists attack America on September 11
2003	War in Iraq

It's never been this bad? As you can see, it has frequently been this bad! We've weathered every conceivable catastrophe, except nuclear war. For instance, the stock market crash in 1987 was supposed to usher in a depression that would make 1929 look like child's play.

At 11:00 a.m. on October 19, 1987, the market was down a little over 200 points, and I remember being in a bit of a state of shock, wondering how low it could go. By the end of the day we had experienced a *508 point decline!* Stocks were decimated; equity in clients' accounts had shrunk precipitously. I knew the next day would be a horrible one. Brokers would have to call their clients with the bad news, and those clients who were unlucky enough to be on margin (when an investor borrows money from the broker to buy stocks) would be faced with the prospect of selling at huge losses or putting up much-needed cash to cover their margin positions.

That evening I saw brokers crying in the parking lot on their way to their cars. It was scary. The real news that day, however, was the threat that the banks wouldn't loan money to New York Stock Exchange members to cover their commitments. Firms had to step up to the plate that day and buy when no one else would—and they did. They bought stock worth roughly $30 billion. Well, $30 billion isn't exactly chump change, and the brokerage firms had to tap their credit lines.

The banks initially balked at loaning the money, and it took some pretty nifty arm twisting by the chairman of the

Federal Reserve to get the banks to front the money. If they hadn't done that, the stock market might have opened at zero the next day.

Let me be quite clear here: the stock market can rival any soap opera for straight drama, and the story of October 19, 1987, is evidence of that.

However, what do I remember most about this historic day? The next day, Tuesday, October 20, *the market went up 140 points*. That's just one of many instances.

So what has the stock market done over the last seventy-five years of turmoil, gloom and doom, and endless prognostications of recession and depression? It's gone up *almost 11 percent* per year on a compounded basis, which means that your money would have doubled every six and a half years! How's that for putting fear to rest?

One has to ask how this kind of stock market performance is possible given the tremendous amount of horrible news. Well, I'm not certain any one answer to that question is right, but I am willing to venture my opinion. I believe that the United States of America's economic system, while flawed, is the best one in the world and that the rest of the world is aware of that. Lest you think this analysis hokey, let me ground this argument in economic terms: Our system works. Other systems, not based on free markets, do not. At least, they don't work as well. The former Soviet Union proves that premise.

Economics is the effective utilization of scarce resources. Now, that's a fancy way of saying that money goes where it is treated best. Let's say that a farmer knows that if he grows corn, he'll sell it at a price that will make him some money. Therefore, he invests in corn. But let's suppose that instead of corn, the government orders him to grow soybeans, where he will earn no profit, only the fixed price that the government will pay him. What incentive does he have to do any more than he needs to barely scrape by? The freedom to choose your product is at the core of

American free enterprise. Centrally planned governments, like the former Soviet Union, never understood this concept. That, no doubt, is why it is the *former* Soviet Union. That country had warehouses full of stuff nobody wanted and huge shortages of food!

Remember when the U.S. had to send the Soviet Union tons and tons of wheat? Didn't you ever wonder why? The communist government had created jobs for people rather than letting them seek their own success. Unfortunately, the cost of that governmental mistake is borne on the backs of the lower class. In short, the people's hope had to rest on the government rather than on their own initiative. That is a prescription for disaster every time.

Hope is at the core of the American system. How many times have we told our children, "You can do and be anything you want to be"? That is hope. You can be the son of an Italian immigrant shoemaker, as I was, and wind up on national television and radio. Is this a great country or what? You betcha, and that's the point.

I come from a generation that in grade school had to practice a drill called "duck and cover"—getting under your desk and putting your head between your legs. Basically, knowing how to do this was supposed to protect school-children in the event of a nuclear attack. We can argue all day about the stupidity of the drill. The point is that we were trying to protect ourselves from an attack emanating from the Soviet Union—a nation that no longer exists.

It wasn't Reagan's Star Wars program that killed the Soviet Union. No, it was a complete economic collapse brought about by the policies of a centralized government that thought party leaders knew what was best for the people. They didn't. Placing power in the hands of people generates hope. Hope activates pricing power. Hope invites initiative. When a father and mother have the knowledge that their children will have the opportunity to blossom as a result of their hard work, they work hard. That is the essence of hope. America is the home of that hope. That is why this system works and why you need not fear investing in it.

Here's the really amazing thing: The rest of the world gets it. But many of us here in America don't.

Lest you think such hope must involve the accumulation of material possessions, let me put that notion to rest. This hope lies not in what you can buy but in *what you can be*. Principle before profit leads to profit every time. That's hope.

I think about my lifetime and all that has transpired. I have already alluded to the demise of the Soviet Union. I never thought I would see that in my lifetime. I think about the fall of the Berlin Wall. I remember so vividly John F. Kennedy standing in the shadow of that wall proclaiming, *"Ich bin ein Berliner."* I remember Ronald Reagan admonishing then Soviet premier Mikhail Gorbachev with the famous words, "Mr. Gorbachev, tear down this wall!" And Gorbachev did. I remember a lone Chinese college student standing in front of a tank in Tiananmen Square, demanding his right to be free. Today China owns the Hong Kong stock exchange, the second largest example of capitalism in the world. Haven't you ever wondered how in the world the Chinese communists ended up with Hong Kong? Do you think they don't understand the power of private ownership?

Here's a prediction: within fifty years, China will overtake the United States as the world's largest economy. With 1.2 billion people starving for goods and services, it's got to happen. Already our largest trade deficit is with the Chinese. We import more of their goods than any other nation does, and we import more from China than from anywhere else in the world. The salient point in all of this is that fighting was not necessary to overcome the Soviet Union. Not a shot was fired, yet the Soviet Union collapsed. In a sense there was a war; it just wasn't fought with missiles.

Muammar Qaddafi, the dictator of Libya, recently admitted and denounced Libya's role in international terrorism. Qaddafi didn't suddenly get religion. The economic conditions in his country got him. The people were getting restless. They needed foreign capital in order to create jobs for the people and to develop their oil reserves—as true an example of the marketplace at work as one will ever see. That is the power of hope.

That is why you need have no fear of America and American industry collapsing. I read with amusement the editorials of those proclaiming the decline of America. Whenever I hear the now-too-familiar refrain of "It's never been this bad," I have to laugh. Let me ask you one question. Have you ever heard of a nation which, having once tasted freedom, ever gave their freedom back?

What's important in this discussion is the reminder that fear has no place in an American investment portfolio. America will succeed because our country is free. America always has. America always will. That's the point. That is why you need have no fear of investing in American companies and resources. America is the noblest economic experiment in the history of humankind. The real mistake in all of this occurs when you don't invest in America and its industry.

One example of this is the saga of International Business Machines (IBM) in 1994. A voracious press had seemed to declare IBM in a coma. The company might not have been fatally ill, but the vital signs weren't great. Well, look at what happened the year after that rather ominous diagnosis.

IBM replaced their chairman of the board, slashed their dividend, slimmed down their product line, and laid off tens of thousands of people. And what was the result? IBM started to stir. Staying with the coma analogy, IBM began to wiggle its toes. The company was about to reclaim the title of being the number one maker of personal computers. As a result, brokerage firms began to recommend buying IBM stock.

At the time of the ominous predictions, the stock went from the high mark of $90 in price to the low mark of $40. However, by 1994 it was at about $50 per share. By March of 1995, IBM was trading at $81.50. And in the early years of the new millennium, IBM stock got as high as $123 per share! That shows you how hard it is to kill a $60 billion American company. If you were a shareholder and kept the faith or perhaps even bought the stock on its way down, you were rewarded.

I am not suggesting for a moment that economic hard times will not come. That's the nature of the bust-to-boom business cycle. I am suggesting that successful investors never forget the outcome of the cycle. It always goes from bust to boom and then back to bust and up to boom. That's the nature of a free market.

Free markets look for efficiency, and when they find it, they turn to it. So yesterday's horse and buggy is tomorrow's Ford Mustang. Progress in a free economy is inexorable, relentless, unforgiving, and, most importantly, inevitable—and this all stems from hope. Consequently, fear is simply an inconvenience to be conquered by the astute investor.

All one need do is wait it out. That's why the simplicity of the buy and hold, broadly diversified strategy over a long period of time works mathematically. The strategy works because the system works. So invest in the system and do not fall victim to the hype. That, my friends, is the first way to conquer fear.

Second, in my own fight against fear, I am constantly reminded of the admonition Jesus most often gave his followers: "Don't be afraid" (Luke 5:10; John 14:27). Obviously fear is a natural part of our human makeup, and Jesus wanted to help us overcome that. We would all do well to listen to Jesus.

But we still have to deal with the other side of the coin: greed.

Antidotes to Greed

Pride lies at the core of greed. Our pride in ourselves is the culprit. When we seek the affirmation of our own greatness, great mistakes are made. Fear can make us hesitant to take advantage of an opportunity. Greed destroys that opportunity, because it forces us to invest at precisely the wrong time, at the highest prices possible.

The first antidote to greed is to recognize this hateful emotion in ourselves. This requires an intellectual honesty that most of us find difficult to acquire. In short, we have to admit to ourselves that we are full of beans. It is in this regard that I am most doubtful and most suspicious of contemporary humanity. Most of us don't want to admit our failures and never will.

Let's look at the telltale signs of the malady. The stock market has increased for a number of years in a row. A new industry has taken over the imagination of the investing public, like high technology did in the 1990s. Or go back a few generations and think of the advent of railroads at the beginning of the industrial revolution or the invention of the car or the airplane. Each signaled new prosperity.

An aura of wealth grips society at those moments, and we sense that we can do nothing wrong ever again. That's greed. Those who recognize it will prosper by not participating. Those who get caught up in the hype and the belief that somehow, someway it's different this time will suffer economic hardship. It's the nature of the business cycle when it returns to the downside.

I don't want you to think that greed is only about the pursuit of stock market profits, either. Here's an actual conversation from my radio broadcast.

One day a woman called my show and said, "Danny, I need your advice. I recently inherited $50,000 from my grandfather, and I want to buy a bigger house in a better part of town for my kids."

123

"How many kids do you have?"

"Four, all under the age of five."

"My, you are busy. What's your household income?"

"About $30,000 per year."

Here there was a pause in our conversation. I was trying desperately to figure out how this family could make ends meet on such a modest income with four kids. Then a thought occurred to me.

"Is that just your income, or you and your husband's income? . . . You are married, right?"

"Yes, I'm married, but I'm a stay-at-home mom. My husband works. We have our eye on a house in the southeast part of town. It's listed at about $250,000, so if we put the $50,000 down, can we afford it?"

"At first blush, I don't think so. But let me make certain I understand exactly what you are telling me. You and your husband have four children, and he earns $30,000 a year. Is that all of your income? Do you have any outside savings or anything like that?"

"No, that's it. My husband is trying to get another job, but he already has two jobs."

"Wait a minute. Your husband has two jobs? Two full-time jobs?"

"Yes."

"So he's already working eighty hours a week, is that right?"

"Yes."

"And he's looking for a third? When does he sleep? Let me ask you this: Why do you want to move to another house? And does it have to be that particular house?"

"It's my dream house. I simply have to have it."

(I thought she wanted it for her kids.)

"The neighborhood is so much nicer, and we would fit in with the people who live there," she explained.

"Ma'am, I have to tell you that I find this conversation unbelievable. You want something you cannot afford, and you are willing to sacrifice your husband to get it. Even worse, your husband, I assume, is willing to make the sacrifice. That's all the bad news. Here's the good news. No bank or mortgage company would approve your mortgage. You can't afford it.

"Now, $50,000 is a lot of money. Why not think of a better use for the money? For instance, how are you going to educate the kids? . . . Do you owe any money?"

"Oh, sure, with four kids, you always owe money."

"Credit cards, cars, what?"

"Both."

"How much do you think you owe?"

"Probably $20,000 to $25,000."

"And you still want that house?"

"Absolutely."

I had to tell the lady that there was no conceivable way I could help her. I don't believe she wanted to be helped. She just wanted that house. She thought it would make her happy. She thought that she could travel in a different social circle, one that she was meant to travel in. That is also pride, and it's fatal. Living beyond your means and wanting even more is clear evidence. When you are consumed with bills and can't stop spending, you've got a pride problem and a greed problem.

The solution to managing your emotions comes from surrendering those emotions to God. Trying to control your own sense of self is a prescription for disaster. It's also very, very tiring. Why not let him do it? You can go on living the way you have been, relying on yourself and trying to solve your own problems, but I have a question for you that I borrowed from the television talk show host Dr. Phil:

How's that working for you so far?

Let me end this chapter by sharing a story I read in *USA Today* many years ago. A trust bought 100 shares of IBM stock in 1928. Now, on the day they bought the stock, a total of 900 shares of IBM were traded. The stock closed at $123 per share. That made the purchase at cost worth $12,300.

The stock was handed down through a trust to various family members and eventually to a home for the aged in California. In 1994, the original 100 shares were worth $4,500,000. That calculates to a 36,600 percent return.

Now, some of you are saying to yourselves, "Sure, Danny, that's great, but if I wait sixty-six years, I'll be the richest 130-year-old guy in the country." While past performance is no guarantee of future results, I would suggest that you are missing the point. Think of all the time that passed between 1928 and 1994 and all of the good news and bad news that occurred during that time period. That stock went through the Great Depression, World War II, Vietnam, and countless recessions, and it still relentlessly appreciated.

That's the point. Stocks go up and they go down. Remember that bad news, whether it be about an individual company or the overall economy, rarely is as bad as it sounds. The same is true, however, for good news. Think logically about the events, apply the healthy doses of common sense to make successful decisions, and then breathe a sigh of relief. You've managed your emotions. You have an opportunity to be a good steward of your resources.

9

TWO THINGS ARE CERTAIN

Retirement Plans and Taxes

How many of you like paying taxes? Do I hear a loud sigh? Or "What a silly question! No one *likes* to pay taxes." Yet we all pay taxes to support our government. And let's be truthful—we also pay taxes because we may either lose everything we have or go to jail if we don't. Some of us even pay taxes because the Bible indicates that we should do so.

Many of us know how the Pharisees tried to trick Jesus by asking the question, "Is it right to pay taxes to the Roman government or not?" (see Matt. 22:15–22). As you can see, taxes were as controversial then as they are now—even more so because the Jews were paying taxes to the Roman conquerors.

In answering the Pharisees' question, Jesus asked them to give him a Roman coin, the currency at that time. Then he asked, "Whose picture and title are stamped on it?" "Caesar's" was the obvious reply.

"Well, then," Jesus said, "give to Caesar what belongs to him" (Matt. 22:21 NLT).

However, we should notice that *this biblical admonition said nothing about paying taxes that we don't have to pay.* Knowing about legal tax deductions is not ducking our obligation to our government. Far from it. That day Jesus went on to say, "But everything that belongs to God must be given to God" (Matt. 22:21 NLT). Taking legal tax deductions is just being a good steward of the Lord's possessions. So we should do everything legally possible to minimize the tax burden placed upon us by the government.

Having established the game plan, one needs to know the rules. I am going to discuss generally what can be done to minimize your tax bite without being too terribly specific regarding the numbers, because the rules change so frequently. For example, I will tell you to contribute to your 401(k) packages at work without telling you all the legal limits that are in place, since they change fairly frequently.

Let me start by repeating a warning I've mentioned earlier: never buy or sell anything just for the tax consideration. The same holds true for *not* buying or selling. For example, the excuse "I don't want to sell a stock because I don't want to pay the capital gains tax" is silly if the price of the stock goes down, especially if it goes down more than the tax would have been. Further, buying a limited partnership (an investment that limits your liability to the amount of the investment) because you can deduct five times the amount of the dollars you invest is equally silly. Invest in stocks that represent quality; if they happen to have a tax benefit, great. But remember, investing in something just for the tax break is one of the seven common mistakes investors make. It sounds great, but the logic is basically wrong.

Delaying taxation is another matter. Let me demonstrate the power of delaying the tax man. Let's suppose that Aunt

Minnie invests $10,000 in a growth mutual fund that averages a 10 percent rate of return for thirty years. For illustration, here's what would happen to that money if Minnie invests in a tax-deferred account like a 401(k) or a variable annuity versus in a regular account where she has to pay taxes on the dividends and the interest each year. And let's assume that Aunt Minnie is in the 20 percent tax bracket. Here's what the investment would look like after thirty years:

Tax Deferred Account	$174,494.02
Taxable Account	$100,626.57

That's the difference between an 8 percent return and a 10 percent return. Which would you rather have? Now, the skeptics will say that this looks great, but you still have to pay Uncle Sam when you take money out of the 401(k) or the variable annuity. That's true, but you can control the taxes at that point and on a much larger amount. The 401(k) has had time to grow so the balance is larger. You don't have to take it all out at once. Most leave as much as they can for as long as they can. (You need the advice of a tax consultant to do so, however.) I always want to pay Uncle Sam later rather than sooner.

Over the entire twenty years of my financial advising career, I have given countless speeches to blue collar employees who typically live paycheck to paycheck. I always advise them to invest in their company's retirement plan. Their lament is always the same: "I can't afford it. I need my money!" And my retort is always the same: "You can't afford not to do it."

Let me illustrate it this way. In America today, most folks eat at McDonald's, or at a McDonald's wannabe, at least once a week. My best guess is that the average Joe probably spends $5 a day on lunch, snacks, or whatever. I'd make a reasonable guess that most people blow five bucks a day on such extras. Well, let's put that five bucks per day in a tax-deferred vehicle for a forty-year working career, compound it at a stock market average return of 10 percent, and see what we get. Remember, we are talking about money that is discretionary. You don't have to spend it. You can save it. What are you throwing away on Big Macs, Slim Jims, and Slurpees? How about $888,504.56? You could *buy* a McDonald's with that kind of money!

Look at that number again. That represents $5 each day, saved every year for forty years, compounded at 10 percent. We throw away almost a million dollars during our working lives. A contribution of five dollars per day for someone making a modest salary of $25,000 per year represents a 7 percent deferral of income. How can anybody *not* afford to do it, given the pot of gold at the end of the rainbow?

With such advantages in mind, let's look at the effect of taxes on retirement savings.

Pension and Retirement

For most people, the company they work for will provide the biggest retirement benefit of all. People who spend most of their working lives with one company, especially if that company is generous in its contributions to an employee savings plan, can accumulate serious wealth investing in these plans. There's one catch. You have to participate to enjoy the benefits.

We can divide retirement savings programs into two types: *defined benefit plans*, where the company promises to pay a defined amount to the employee upon retirement, and *defined contribution plans*, where the company promises to donate a certain amount to the employee's retirement. In the case of defined contribution plans, the employee is allowed to participate as well, often on a pre-tax basis.

Many of us in the baby boom generation grew up watching our parents work for one company for most of their working lives, hoping to retire with a generous company pension. My own father worked for a company for forty-six years. When he retired, he received a check for $226 each month until he died. That money came from his company's defined benefit plan.

Let's begin our discussion of the effect of taxes on retirement savings by talking about the defined benefit plan.

The Traditional Pension Plan: The Defined Benefit Plan

Did you ever wonder where the idea of a pension came from? Would you be surprised that the idea was first proposed by a religious group? That's right, according to Jordan Goodman, author of *Everyone's Money Book*, "The idea of an employer providing a retirement pension plan for its employees started in the United States in 1759 when the Presbyterian Church created a fund to care for the widows and children of ministers."[1]

Here's the basic idea. A company sets aside a certain amount of money and isolates it in segregated accounts for each employee each year. The company then invests the money (hopefully wisely). When Aunt Minnie retires, the company pays her a monthly benefit, the amount of which is based on her years of service. The company gets a tax break by taking a deduction when it sets the contribution aside, and the money grows tax-free until it's paid out to Aunt Minnie, who is then taxed at ordinary income tax rates.

Now, to qualify for the monthly benefit, Aunt Minnie has to work at the company long enough to become *vested*. The company sets the standards for this. How long is long enough? The company decides that. For example, let's say that the company determines that in order to become fully vested in the company pension plan, each employee must complete five years of service. The company sets aside the contribution on Aunt Minnie's behalf, and she quits after four years. Aunt Minnie was not vested, based on the company's requirements, so she loses her benefit.

Suppose, however, the company chooses to partially vest the contributions over the same five-year period. Let's say that the plan sets a vesting schedule over five years and vests 20 percent each year. The company sets aside the contribution on Aunt Minnie's behalf, and she quits after four years. This time, because of the vesting schedule, Aunt Minnie will eventually receive 80 percent of the contribution (within five years of eligibility, 20 percent each year for four years).

PAYMENT METHODS

How do you get paid from the defined benefit pension plan when you retire? Well, most companies use one of three methods:

- *The flat benefit formula* pays a fixed amount each month upon retirement. The longer you worked, the higher the payment.
- *The career average formula plan* does just what its name implies. It averages the income the employee earned over his or her entire career. The company pays you a percentage of your pay for every year you participated in the pension plan. You get to choose whether you want to take it in a monthly benefit or a one-time payment. Typically the employer averages your salary over a designated time frame, for example, the last five years that you worked.
- *The final pay method* takes into consideration the last years of your career when you were probably making the most money. Once employees retire under this method, they receive a percentage of their final pay,

multiplied by the number of years they worked, in a monthly benefit or a one-time payment (again, the employee gets to choose).

Notice how important your age is in these methods. Typically, if you retire at a younger age, your benefit is reduced. If you wait to retire, your benefit can be maximized. But the plans have to pay you when you reach age 70½. That's the only way the government can secure a tax payment from the plan. Remember, these funds have been allowed to accumulate tax free. Only when the company pays it to you does the IRS receive its pound of flesh.

INVESTING THE MONEY FROM A DEFINED BENEFIT PLAN

Up until retirement, employees haven't had any say in how the money in their pension plan has been handled. However, at the point of distribution, the employee takes the reins. Deciding how to take your money is an important decision, and you have two different options: an annuity or a lump sum.

Annuities. An annuity is an insurance contract that allows the investor to receive regular monthly checks at a fixed rate. Typically the longer you elect to receive the payments, the smaller the payment will be. The challenge comes when you face a basic question as you make this decision: How long do you think you are going to live? Let's look at some choices.

- *Ten year term certain.* If you think your lifespan is less than ten years, this might be the way to go. This option provides the highest benefit but also can hurt you if you survive longer than ten years. This is a roll of the dice unless you are absolutely certain your health will give out within that time frame. If it does not, you could run out of money.

133

- *Life annuity with ten year term certain.* This pays you for-ever, but if you die before you have received benefits for ten years, your beneficiary will only get the rest of the ten-year benefits. Obviously, this is riskier for your spouse than for you. This policy pays a smaller benefit than the ten year term certain option, since you are insured for life. The key here is to make sure that your beneficiary (usually your spouse) has enough resources to live on after his or her ten-year payments expire.

- *Life annuity.* This option pays you until you die. The payments are significantly reduced from the other op-tions, but you are guaranteed an income for life. How-ever, the benefits stop once you die. Your beneficiary gets nothing after your death.

- *Joint and survivor annuity.* This may be the best option if you are married and someone else depends on your income. This pays both you and your surviving spouse until you both die. Typically the payments that the spouse receives after your death are less than the benefit you receive while you are alive, but at least some income is provided for the remainder of his or her life.

Lump sum. Some companies might let you take your re-tirement in one fell swoop, called a lump-sum distribution. Now, this might seem attractive if you fancy yourself an astute, disciplined investor. You might be able to do better by taking the lump sum and investing it over a long period of time. Of course, you also run the risk of losing your money if you are not particularly gifted as an investor.

If you are going to take advantage of this offer, I would counsel you to seek professional help as you invest those funds. Once you get that lump sum in one check, you have the option of rolling it over into another qualified plan like an Individual Retirement Account (IRA). Now, pay careful attention. If you do not roll over that lump-sum distribution within sixty days, the entire amount becomes subject to ordinary income tax rates. In addition, if you take the benefit before age 59½, the distribution could be subject to an additional 10 percent IRS penalty.

Make absolutely certain that the lump-sum check is not sent to you. Have the check sent directly from your company's pension plan into the IRA account at your bank, brokerage, or mutual fund. This could be a huge mistake if not handled properly. The lump-sum option may seem desirable since it probably represents the most money you have ever seen at one time. However, for that reason, it carries big responsibility. Make certain you have taken the time to contemplate your future career plans, using your future income needs as a key barometer. This is no time to flex your muscles. *Get help!*

Taxes can bite you big time on this decision since many complex rules govern lump-sum distributions. You might consider five-year forward averaging if you are over age 59½. Five-year forward averaging lets you spread out the tax payments over a five-year period of time instead of paying all of the taxes in the year you take the lump sum. But how can you consider it if you don't even know the option exists on lump-sum distributions? So, I repeat, *get help!*

Unfunded Pension Plans

Much has been written lately about companies that have defined benefit pension plans set up but then do not have the funds to meet the payments because of bad business decisions. What's an employee to do? Prior to 1974, there was no redress. If the company went bankrupt, the employee was out of luck. In 1974, Congress passed the Employee Retirement Income Security Act (ERISA), which has become the standard for retirement law. ERISA guidelines require

135

companies that offer pension plans to contribute enough each year to pay for the cost.

However, a company can still experience a tough year and not have enough to make the payment. The company can apply for a waiver for that year, but benefit obligations carry over. In other words, if the employer can't make the payment this year, the company makes a double payment next year. Well, this sounds great in theory, but many companies are significantly underfunded because of sustained business declines. For this reason, a company could still go bankrupt with an outstanding pension obligation that it cannot meet.

Again, the government comes to the rescue in this type of situation. A government agency called the Pension Benefit Guaranty Corporation (PBGC), established within ERISA, acts like insurance, much as the Federal Deposit Insurance Corporation (FDIC) does for banks and the Securities Investors Protective Corporation (SIPC) does for brokerage firms.

The PBGC takes over your pension payments but only covers basic benefits, so don't expect to get rich at the expense of the government. They'll cover the pension payment and adjust it each year to a maximum amount, but that's it. Don't expect the PBGC to be bound by cost of living increases or any of the other goodies your private pension plan promised you.

Defined benefit plans like those described above are a good thing. Anything a company is willing to give you simply because you work there is a good thing. There is a fly in the ointment, though. Typically, many companies will take a risk-averse approach because they have a fiduciary responsibility to invest this money on the employee's behalf. This risk-averse approach often results in a low rate of return. For example, instead of investing in the stock market and taking the chance of losing principal, an employer might invest in a fixed annuity for a guaranteed low rate of return.

This could significantly impact an employee's final benefit. The strategy is safer for the employer but less advantageous over the long run for the employee.

In the world of investment, a defined benefit plan is not necessarily considered a great investment. These types of plans put employers in a very precarious, contentious position in that they serve as a kind of surrogate parent for the retired employee. For instance, what if the company doesn't handle the investments within the plan very well, which results in lower payouts? Or worse, what if the company defined the benefit to be paid and then cannot pay that amount?

Defined benefit plans are being replaced in popularity with defined contribution plans. These plans spread the risk between the employers and the employees so each bears some responsibility for the ultimate result. These contribution plans are popular for other reasons as well. For example, in today's society, most folks change jobs much more frequently than in previous generations. Contribution plans are portable. In most cases when you leave one company you can transfer your company contribution plan into your new company's plan or into an individual retirement account.

An investor can always do better by having flexibility within the vehicle. That leads us to our next discovery: the defined contribution pension plan.

The Defined Contribution Pension Plan

The main difference between the defined benefit plan and the defined contribution plan lies in the area of responsibility. Now the employer and the employee share the responsibility, as I mentioned earlier. However, the opportunity for significant capital accumulation is much greater with the defined contribution plan since an employee lawsuit is much less likely.

Along with the employee's increased reward comes substantial personal responsibility to manage the assets. You have many more choices to make. How big a contribution should you make? What investments should you place your money into and in what percentages? And along with those choices comes the possibility of making poor choices that result in a loss of your money.

In this plan employers can make contributions based on profitability. The better the firm does, the higher their contribution can be. The firm can also contribute absolutely nothing if they have a bad year. Or an employer can set up and maintain a plan but not make contributions. However, most defined contribution pension plans involve a combination of contributions from both the employer and the employee. At the end of your career, you can roll the money over or convert it into an annuity to provide an income.

Defined contribution plans take different forms. They can be employee stock ownership plans (ESOPs), money-purchase pension plans, profit-sharing plans, salary reduction type programs such as 401(k)s or 403(b)s, stock bonus plans, or thrift plans. Let's look at these six types of defined contribution plans.

The employee stock ownership plan (ESOP). This is basically a profit-sharing plan. The firm's contributions and your contributions are both invested in the company's stock. This could serve as terrific motivation to work diligently. Of course, you had better believe in the future prospects of your company, because in effect you are putting all your retirement eggs in your company's stock basket.

The money-purchase pension plan. This plan gives your company no way out. The employer has to contribute the same set amount of your salary each year, regardless of company performance. When you retire, you get a monthly benefit based on how much has been accumulated.

The profit-sharing plan. This plan is like a money-purchase pension plan in that the firm contributes a set amount of your salary, but it is dependent on whether or not the firm made any money. It can be as much as 15 to 20 percent of your income in a good year or nothing if the firm actually makes nothing or loses money.

However, for morale purposes the company can decide to keep the employees happy during a tough year by making a contribution. The flexibility of this option is that the contributions can be invested in a widely diversified portfolio, including company stock, bonds, mutual funds, real estate, and insurance.

The salary reduction plan—a 401(k) or 403(b). The most common vehicle used today for retirement savings is the company savings plan commonly known as a 401(k). Have you ever wondered why it's called that? It's simple, really. The term 401(k) comes from the IRS tax code that sets up the rules and regulations overseeing the program.

The salary reduction plan allows employees to defer a percentage of their salaries on a pre-tax basis and place it in a tax-deferred account to invest in a widely diversified portfolio of investment choices. When this is done in a corporation, it's called a 401(k). When it's done in a non-profit organization, like a church or a school, it's called a 403(b). These are terrific retirement choices, given the multiple benefits.

First of all, the deferral is done on a pre-tax basis, meaning that every dollar you choose to place in the program is a dollar less earned in salary and therefore a dollar that is not available to the government for income tax. If you are in a 30 percent tax bracket, every dollar you place into a 401(k) or a 403(b) automatically saves you 30 cents in taxes.

This pre-tax benefit is very, very attractive compared to other types of plans which rely on post-tax dollars, effectively causing you to pay tax twice on the same money. Additionally, the company may provide a matching contribution which can be very rewarding. While the employer may not match your contributions dollar for dollar, anything that the company contributes on your behalf is found money. Let me ask you this: if you were walking down the street and you saw a dollar bill lying on the sidewalk, would you pick it up? My guess is that you would. That's a picture of participating in a 401(k) or a 403(b) with a company that matches contributions.

Second, the money grows tax-deferred. You don't pay any tax on the money until you pull it out of the plan, presumably many years later when your income is lower and therefore your rate of tax is lower. Remember, pay taxes later if at all possible.

Now, you have to be careful how you take money out of these plans. The IRS will penalize withdrawals before age 59½ as well as tax you. You also have to be careful how you transfer these kinds of assets if you leave one company for another. Aside from a few exceptions like buying a home for the first time or a medical hardship, the government doesn't want you to take money out of your retirement program until you have to, for fear that you might never replace that money. These plans are not passbook savings programs. They are meant to be invested over the long, long term. That is what provides the opportunity for substantial wealth accumulation. While you can borrow from these plans, I would recommend that you don't. Again, retirement dollars need to be accumulated for that specific purpose. Borrowing leaves open the possibility that you never pay the money back. It's gone forever.

The stock bonus plan. This is like a profit-sharing plan in that bonuses are paid when the company makes a lot of money. When you retire, you get the stock, not the cash.

The thrift savings plan. This is an interesting option. Employees can contribute a certain percentage of their salaries on an after-tax basis. The money can be invested in stocks, bonds, fixed income investments like guaranteed investment contracts (GICs, which act like a CD), or money funds. The corporation can choose to match contributions or not. Usually any money that the company contributes has to go into company stock, so that is a bit of a drawback.

VESTING

The vesting rules for defined contribution plans are quite different from those for defined benefit plans. Remember, you may have to wait quite a few years to be vested in your company's traditional pension plan. But the contributions you make to a defined contribution plan are immediately vested. Your money is always your money, and it is safe from the company's creditors as well. If you leave the company, it goes with you.

However, this does not apply to the company's contributions. You can lose some or all of the match if you leave. There is a method to this madness. The company is trying to keep you at the company. By making you wait for the contributions to vest, you may decide to stick it out just to get that money. If you reach normal retirement age with a company, the company's contributions are yours to keep, regardless of how long you have been with that company.

THE BENEFITS OF DEFINED CONTRIBUTION PLANS

You can probably tell by now that I am a huge, huge fan of participation in a defined contribution retirement plan. I highly recommend that you consider investing in a defined contribution plan for the following reasons:

1. Whenever you can invest automatically, you don't miss the money.
2. Dollar cost averaging (buying more shares when prices are down and fewer shares when prices are up) is forced because you invest the same amount each time

in the same instrument. Over time, dollar cost averaging causes an overall lower cost of shares.
3. You pay no commissions.
4. The company match is found money.
5. You get lots of choices and can move between them easily.
6. For many, this represents the best chance to accumulate significant assets.
7. If need be, you can borrow from the plans at lower than market rates.

I have seen tremendous amounts of money accumulated in these plans during my time in the financial services industry. I am talking about hundreds of thousands of dollars. Most people could never hope to save that much money with traditional savings methods. If you have a 401(k) or 403(b) available to you, invest in it to the max!

I mentioned the tax benefit earlier. Let me demonstrate it to you in the following example. Assuming a $50,000 salary, a 6 percent pre-tax contribution, and a thirty-cent-on-the-dollar company match, here's how much tax you can save per year:

	Plan	No Plan
Salary	$50,000	$50,000
Pre-tax contribution	3,000	0
Salary reported to IRS	47,000	50,000
Minus federal income tax (30% tax bracket)	−14,100	−15,000
Take home pay	32,900	35,000
Taxes saved (paid $15,000 in tax versus $14,100)	900	0
Company contribution ($.30 x 3,000)	900	0
Total Savings	$1,800	0

Please note that this example doesn't even include savings in state and local taxes or Social Security taxes. Also, the earnings on the $3,000 investment are allowed to grow tax-deferred, so that means even further tax savings.

THE FURTHER IMPACT OF TAX DEFERRAL

When you mix the advantages of tax-deferred compounded savings and the power of the company matching contribution, the results can significantly outperform what you could do on your own with after-tax dollars. Look at the following illustration prepared by Greenwich Associates of Greenwich, Connecticut, using the following assumptions:

1. You begin contributing to a defined contribution plan at age twenty-five when you earn an annual salary of $25,000. Every year your salary rises by 4 percent to keep pace with inflation.
2. You contribute 6 percent of your salary to the plan each year, and your employer matches fifty cents on the dollar.
3. You invest half the money in stocks and half in bonds, achieving a long-term average return of 9 percent.
4. You would have paid a 30 percent federal income tax rate on your savings outside the plan. This applies when you take the money out at age sixty-five, which is when you are in this higher bracket.
5. You retire at age sixty-five.

In this scenario, you would accumulate $1,315,944. Even with no company match, you would accumulate $877,926. If you had gotten the employer match of fifty cents on the dollar but it was taxed, you would end up with $709,167. And if you saved exactly the same amount of money and earned the same return over the entire forty years but received no employer match and enjoyed no tax savings, you would have accumulated $472,778. By investing in the salary reduction program, you would have $800,000 more without ever having increased your percentage of savings![2] Now, think about the people who have said to me, "But Danny, I need my money!"

Allocating Assets in Your Retirement Investments

The important thing to remember when approaching how to diversify your retirement investments is to take into consideration all of your assets, both those inside qualified plans and those outside. One school of thought suggests that your retirement funds ought to be invested much more safely than non-retirement assets. I don't really believe that it matters, as long as your asset allocation takes into consideration all your assets. Within that framework, I don't have a problem with using your retirement assets as the safer part of your total investments. For example, if you have a 60 percent growth, 40 percent fixed asset allocation, I have no problem with using the 401(k) for the 40 percent of the allotment.

However, you should consider the positive tax advantage inherent inside your retirement plan. If you can get 10 percent inside a tax-advantaged vehicle, that's better than 10 percent outside of one. You can also buy growth and income stocks so that taxable dividends end up tax deferred. When you invest in growth stocks, you are only taxed if you sell them later with a capital gain. Therefore, if you are going to hold growth stocks for a long time, you don't necessarily need the tax shelter offered by the defined contribution plan.

Another school of thought in this regard says that a salary reduction plan is the perfect place to achieve maximum capital gains over a long time. If you begin investing in a 401(k) at an early age, the likelihood of a high return is pretty good. Therefore, I won't quibble about this. Some of this has to do with your own senses and abilities. If you

144

have a personal financial advisor, make certain that he or she is in the loop regarding your retirement savings plans. Who better to know your entire situation and advise accordingly? Who better to know your tolerance for risk? Make no mistake; you must factor in your tolerance for risk before determining how to position your assets inside the retirement plan. It's crucial.

I must warn you about putting too much of your retirement dollars into your company stock. With the decline of the stocks of Enron, WorldCom, US Air, and Duke Energy, this advice is particularly timely. Even if you believe that your company and its management hung the moon, you must fight the temptation to load up with just one stock. Take advantage of the options to diversify. The danger is just too great in this day and age. Your retirement plan could be just one adverse corporate announcement away from being cut in half. Who among us can afford that kind of hit?

For some general allocations for your retirement plan, I urge you to go back to chapter 7 and study the various recipes for Fontana Soufflé. While not precise, they are helpful in determining how much you ought to have where at various times during your working career.

Getting Money Out of a 401(k) Once You Retire

When you retire and are ready to take money out of your 401(k), you basically have three choices: You can take a lump sum. You can keep the funds inside the plan but not contribute any further. Or you can buy an insurance company annuity with the pension plan funds that would provide you an income for a specific period of time.

Taking the lump sum. Let me just be clear about this. Do *not* take all your funds at once unless you intend to roll the funds into an IRA. The taxes will kill you. If you have more than $750,000, the taxes will not only kill you, they will also dismember you. Make certain that you consult a tax professional and get advice as to how to minimize your tax bite when it comes to terminating a pension plan.

Buying an annuity. This option is a little more complicated, given the choices you would have to make. I covered most of those choices earlier in this chapter when I discussed how to use them in the defined benefit plan. Those choices exist for defined contribution plans as well.

Buying a life annuity. Another option is a life annuity with a cash refund. With this annuity you receive guaranteed annuity payments for the rest of your life. But if you die before receiving at least as much as your employer paid for the annuity, your beneficiary (probably your spouse) would be entitled to the difference between the money you had already received and the amount the company paid for the annuity. Obviously, the monthly payments would be lower than an annuity without guarantees.

But What If You Work for Yourself?

Most of the pension plan programs discussed in this chapter are relevant if you work for a larger, established company. But what if you work for yourself? Can you enjoy the benefits of pre-tax contributions with tax deferral options as well? Certainly. You just have to know what vehicle to use. Once again, the advice of a competent advisor is essential in order to determine what you and your company need. Basically you have three options: a Simplified Employee Pension, a Keogh Plan, or an Individual Retirement Account.

Simplified Employee Pensions (SEPs)

You can set up this type of plan for a company with twenty-five or fewer employees, but at least half of them must participate. An SEP is like a defined contribution plan, but it's simpler than a 401(k) since the reporting to the IRS and the Department of Labor is not as troublesome.

Basically, the company sets up an Individual Retirement Account known as an (SEP) IRA for each employee. The employee has to have been an employee for at least three of the last five years and earned a minimum amount of wages (adjusted each year for inflation). The SEP can be funded by the company, the employee, or a combination.

With an SEP, contributions cannot exceed $30,000 in one year, and the employee contribution is limited to about one third of that amount (indexed to inflation) or 15 percent of your wages, whichever is less. Like any other defined contribution plan, the contribution can be pre-tax and thus avoid federal, state, local, and Social Security taxes. So you get the tax benefit in the year you contribute. Also, the SEP qualifies for tax deferral, since it is a qualified pension plan under IRS rules.

Here's a really neat feature: any amount that your company contributes on your behalf is immediately vested. It's yours, and the company can never take it away. You can roll it over when you change jobs as well. Of course, if you take an early withdrawal (before age 59½), you suffer the 10 percent IRS penalty and the current taxation. Just like the other plans, you *must* start to take withdrawals at age 70½.

One drawback (although I think it's really a good thing) is that you cannot borrow funds from an SEP.

Keogh Plans

You don't hear much about Keogh plans anymore. The Keogh was set up in 1962, principally to benefit full-time, self-employed business owners. However, it's also good for people who moonlight, earning extra money in their spare time. They can set up a Keogh.

You can invest up to $30,000 per year, but only if you make less than $150,000 per year. The contribution has to be in the account by December 31 of each year, and the money is post-tax dollars, although you can deduct your contribution on your tax return. Now, that's a significant benefit. You get growth through the tax deferral, and the current tax benefit through the deduction can be substantial.

Like the other plans, you can't draw your money out early without penalties. You can take your investment in a lump sum, but the taxes will kill you, so most folks opt to roll it into an IRA or buy an annuity.

If you are the only one in the plan (as most are), then you cannot borrow against the Keogh. You can invest in individual stocks, bonds, or mutual funds—virtually the whole gamut of investment.

This is a great tool if you have a full-time job and do some work on the side. You can participate in your company's 401(k) or defined benefit plan and also set up a Keogh. Now that's bang for the buck!

Individual Retirement Accounts (IRAs)

From 1981 to 1986, the IRA was the be-all and end-all for the investor. This plan was so popular that Congress passed a law to stop some people from investing in the IRA since the tax coffers were going down as people took advantage of the tremendous tax benefits of the Individual Retirement Account.

Here's a question I get all the time: Why should I invest in an IRA if I'm one of the people who can't deduct it? The answer is obvious. The tax deferral on the accumulated earnings is very, very powerful. The amazing thing to me is the power of the words *tax deduction*. Even though tax-deferred compounding still results in huge tax savings, the amount of money that went into IRAs after 1986 plummeted simply because Congress took away the tax deduction feature for most folks. They never took away the ability for an IRA to grow tax deferred, and yet Americans, in their infinite wisdom, walked away from that!

Even if you never make a contribution to an IRA, open an IRA account. It will come in handy if you change jobs and have to roll over your plan. Now, as much as I like IRAs, understand that a company-sponsored pension plan should be your first choice because of the double whammy it provides. So maximize your contributions into your 401(k) or 403(b) or your defined benefit plan. Only after that consider opening an IRA and contributing to it with post-tax dollars. First things always come first. In the world of retirement planning, IRAs are last. They are still very good, but the other options take precedence.

Here's the best of all worlds: You work for a company and contribute the maximum to your 401(k), and your company makes the maximum match. You have a side job, so you open a Keogh and contribute to that (remember, you can't make more than $150,000 in order to do this). Then you open an IRA and contribute the max to that. That, folks, is retirement planning!

While the rules have changed, the IRA survives and still offers some very attractive features. First of all, even if you have a defined benefit or a defined contribution plan, an SEP or a Keogh, you can still open an IRA. How do you like them apples?

Here's the bad thing. In order to contribute to an IRA, you have to have a job. Contributions can only come from earned income (wages on your W-2 and 1099 forms). That means that dividends and interest don't count. You must have worked in the year you are making the contribution.

While Congress took away the deductibility of the contributions for most people back in 1986, you may be able to deduct all or part of the contribution if you meet certain criteria. For instance, no matter how much money you made on the job, you can deduct up to $2,250 if you are not a participant in an employer's retirement plan. That means you can't work full time or part time for a company that offers a defined benefit or defined contribution plan, even if you do not participate in the plan. If you are working, you can invest up to $2,000. Now, if your spouse earns less than $250, the two of you can contribute $2,250 combined ($2,000 for you and $250 for your spouse).

However, if your income falls within certain limits, you might be able to deduct your IRA contributions even if you are an active participant in a company-sponsored pension plan. Confused yet? As I suggested earlier, consult a financial advisor in order to understand all of this gobbledygook. Oh, and be sure to thank your congressman for the easy-to-read instructions.

Anyway, if you earn less than $25,000 as a single person or $40,000 as a married couple filing jointly, you can deduct your full IRA contribution up to $2,000. If, as a single person, you report adjusted gross income between $25,000 and $35,000, the amount you can deduct is phased out by $1 for each $5 of income above $25,000. For example, if you are single and earn $30,000, you can deduct $1,000 toward an IRA contribution. The same phase-out applies to married couples making between $40,000 and $50,000. For every buck over $40,000, reduce the deductibility by $.50 up to $50,000. So, if you are married and make $45,000, you can deduct $1,000. *Capisce?* If you earn more than $35,000 as a single or $50,000 as a married couple, your IRA contributions are not tax deductible.

Now let's look at tax-advantaged retirement investments that you can purchase outside of your retirement plans.

Municipal Bonds—Tax-Advantaged Retirement Investments

Municipal bonds are probably the most misunderstood investment vehicle out there. First of all, they are bonds. That means you receive interest, just like taxable bonds (such as United States government bonds and bonds issued by corporations). The difference is that the interest from a municipal bond is tax free. In fact, all bonds are free from federal tax. Some are even state and local tax free. The point is, not all tax-free bonds have the same advantage. Bonds not taxable by your state of residence are known as double tax free, and those also not taxed by a locality are triple tax free.

Now, one might ask, how in the world is it possible to not have to pay the federal government their pound of flesh? Well, that's a great question, and to answer it, a little history is in order. In the 1800s the states wanted to borrow money from their citizens in order to build roads and schools and railroads and whatever else tickled their fancy. In order to attract that money, they wanted to give their investors a little sweetener. They thought, *How about if our investors don't have to pay any federal taxes on the money they loan us?* The result was tax-free municipal bonds, which were instituted in 1895 when the United States Supreme Court ruled that the federal government could not interfere with the states' ability to borrow money.

The tax-free bond market is very large, but it's not all that easy to buy and sell bonds. First of all, you need a broker since bonds have no central marketplace like stocks have. Second, these bonds have minimum purchase requirements; usually muni's (as they are called) sell in blocks of five $1,000 bonds. You can buy less, but brokers don't like dealing with less than five bonds. The best thing for investors is to buy the bonds with the idea that they don't want to sell them until the bonds reach maturity. This is because the market has very little trading activity since so few bonds are issued by individual localities.

Here's the danger in buying municipal bonds. Because they are very attractive to investors, very often the issuing parties will place covenants on the bonds, allowing investors to redeem these bonds early if interest rates become favorable. For instance, suppose you buy a municipal bond issued by the state of North Carolina with a promise to pay you 5 percent interest, free from federal and state tax, for ten years. But then interest rates drop so that North Carolina can go into the market and reissue those bonds at 3 percent. What do you think would happen? You guessed it. North Carolina will decide to pay off the 5 percent bondholders with the money they receive from new 3 percent bondholders. In effect, North Carolina promised to pay you for ten years but only paid you for three before they redeemed. Your bonds were "called away" from you because of the change in the marketplace. Investors should check the "call features" of any tax-free bond they are thinking about purchasing.

Another consideration should be the type of tax-free bond being issued. They come in two kinds: general obligation bonds and revenue bonds. A general obligation bond issued by a state or locality has to pay you from their general fund. But a revenue bond's interest payment to you has a contingency—the project that benefits from your money must generate enough revenue to pay you.

For example, say a state borrows money from you to build a highway. The highway generates no revenues, so the state is going to pay the interest to you from their general fund. That's a general obligation bond. On the other hand, if a city decides to borrow money from you to build a hospital, that hospital needs to generate enough revenue to pay your interest. That's a revenue bond. Which is safer? Well, since states have the ability to raise taxes to meet their obligations (called full faith and value), the promise coming from the state is more reliable than the potential for the hospital to turn a profit. For that reason, a general obligation bond pays less interest than a revenue bond, since it is perceived as being less of a risk.

Let me state the obvious: municipal bonds are for people who pay too much in taxes. The average income earner will probably do better in the taxable market.

10

ALL THAT STUFF—IT'S NOT REALLY YOURS

Stewardship

Nothing you possess is yours. Go look in your garage. That car doesn't belong to you. Walk through your house or apartment. What you see isn't yours. Not the dishes, the forks, the napkins, the furniture—nothing. Not the clothes. Not the water in the swimming pool. It all belongs to the Lord. The mailbox is his. The mail is even his, including the bills! (And you thought there was no benefit to being a Christian?) Even your children are gifts from God.

I'm not sure why, but most people struggle with this most basic of biblical concepts. I suspect it's a control issue. We human beings are the ultimate control freaks. We *must* control our "stuff." Why is it so hard to grasp that what we have is not our own? Are we silly enough to imagine that when we face the Day of Judgment, our salvation ultimately depends upon how big our house was?

The answer has to be a resounding "No!" doesn't it?

So let's begin by accepting this statement: What human beings think matters in this world doesn't count for anything in the next. Therefore, the pretense of ownership is simply that: a false assumption based on an illogical belief.

Here's the next bit of bad news. That big job you have? You had nothing to do with it. You are where you are by the grace of God. He did it. Not you. The money you get from your job? Not yours. His. A loan from Almighty God. And he's watching what you do with it.

King David, that kid who killed the giant Goliath and later became king of Israel during the nation's time of greatest glory, said it this way:

> Yours, O LORD, is the greatness, the power, the glory, the victory, and the majesty. Everything in the heavens and on earth is yours, O LORD, and this is your kingdom. We adore you as the one who is over all things. Riches and honor come from you alone, for you rule over everything. Power and might are in your hand, and it is at your discretion that people are made great and given strength.
>
> 1 Chronicles 29:11–12 NLT

I can't tell you how many disasters have hit my clients over the years that can be traced directly to a horrible decision they made based on what they thought was prudent. If they had merely looked to the proper decision maker, all would have been salvaged.

Take, for instance, a golfing friend of mine who usually seems so calm. He credits his peace to his belief in Jesus Christ. Yet every year we have a conversation about his business. He owns a pretty successful but fairly new company that's doing very well on the revenue side. But like the owner of any new business, he is constantly worried about cash flow. Our yearly conversation goes something like this:

"Danny, I'm kinda worried about business. I need permanent financing or I'm not going to make my payroll," he says as we are rounding the ninth hole on our golf cart. "What do you think I should do?"

"Have you prayed about it?" I ask.

"Sure, I have. But I still need to make the payroll."

"Are you reading the Bible every day?"

"No," he admits.

"Have you given the problem to the Lord?"

"Danny, the Lord's not gonna make my payroll."

"Wanna bet?"

My friend thinks that if he just works harder, if he just increases the revenues so that he can positively flow his cash, the problem will be solved. He quotes the parable of the talents (Matt. 25:14–29) to me and implies that being a good steward of his money means that he must work harder. I believe in hard work, but the Bible clearly states that the Lord will provide what we need if we ask for his help.

My friend's problem is not that he is a poor steward. It's that he is trying to solve the problem by *himself*. By doing so, he places himself before God. Trust that the solution rests in the Lord, not in making the payroll.

Yet my friend is partly right when he quotes the parable of the talents. God calls us to be good stewards of what we possess. Just exactly what does that mean? *Webster's* defines *stewardship* as "the individual's responsibility to manage his life and property with proper regard to the rights of others."[1] I believe that faithfulness—being true to God's plan for us—is a part of this. The apostle Paul told the Corinthians, "Now it is required that those who have been given a trust must prove faithful" (1 Cor. 4:2).

I think that I was being faithful when I heard the Lord call me to leave my six-figure job at the bank to open a brokerage firm, write books, give speeches, and do a radio and television show. The genesis of those conversations lie in Scripture; specifically Luke 18:18–29, the story of the rich young ruler. A young ruler asked Jesus what he needed to do to inherit eternal life. Jesus told him to follow the Ten Commandments. The rich guy said that wasn't a problem—he had been doing that his whole life. Jesus then said to sell everything and give the money to the poor, and he would have treasure in heaven.

The young fellow could not do that. Well, that's what I heard God tell me to do. Leave my cushy life to follow him and establish his kingdom in the secular world. I obeyed because I believe disobeying would have meant being unfaithful to God's will.

I believe that faith is trust, but not in myself. Stewardship requires faith in an appropriate outcome: a belief that all will work to the Lord's satisfaction. Second, stewardship requires the implementation of a game plan.

Here's my version of the play book for good stewardship: avoid debt, work hard, train your children, spend wisely, practice absolute honesty, and be a generous and joyful giver. Six biblical precepts. Let's look at each of them individually.

Precept 1: Avoid Debt

Take it from me, stay out of debt. Remember the Shubooties fiasco. None of us wants to dig ourselves out of the financial trouble I faced.

Pay off your credit cards each month. Pay cash for as much as you can. And make your only debt your home mortgage and one car payment—just one car payment.

If you have debt at this time, rest assured, you not only can get out of debt, you can invest and save at the same time. I did it, so I know it can be done. But first you must determine not to incur any further debt than you already have. And once you are out of debt, don't ever get into it again.

Now, getting out of debt is a subject for an entire book, one I expect to write someday in the future. For now you need to ask yourself a question: "Am I replacing the love of God with the love of stuff?" That's what creates the debt problem.

The concept is not new, but I can think of no basic biblical precept that is more commonly misunderstood. Whenever human beings place themselves before God, especially in their desire for material comfort, the game has already been lost before the first pitch. No doubt there may appear to be an early lead in the first few innings, but the outcome is never seriously questioned.

In the movie *Rudy*, the title character desires to play football for the University of Notre Dame. Sadly, he doesn't have the grades to gain admittance. Upon the advice of a kindly priest, he enrolls in a community college and excels in his studies over two full years.

Yet he still fails to gain admittance. Desperate, he turns to the priest one last time for help getting in. If he doesn't make it this time, his dream to play football for the Fighting Irish will die.

The priest explains to Rudy that he is powerless in the situation. "Son, after twenty-five years in the priesthood, I know of only two absolute truths. One, there is a God; and two, I'm not him." Sadly, I think most of us, whether we realize it or not, think that we are God and that we can control our own lives. And therein lies the problem.

This is especially true in the world of finance. I want each of you to answer another question with just one caveat—you must answer truthfully. *Why do people borrow money to purchase material goods?*

The answer to that question gets to the core of financial difficulty and I think reflects the lack of spirituality in our lives. It's also a light to the solution of debt if we are willing to honestly evaluate our individual intent. We buy creature comforts *because we think we deserve them*. We are, after all, gods, are we not? We seek to please ourselves as if we are. The apostle Paul would agree with me. He writes, "There is no one righteous, not even one; there is no one who understands, no one who seeks God" (Rom. 3:10–11).

Even more puzzling are human reactions to the suggestion that we don't own our stuff. People are likely to show anger, defensiveness, and sadness at the suggestion that what's in their closets or their garages doesn't belong to them. But remember, it's just "stuff."

Precept 2: Work Hard

Doesn't everybody think they work hard? I think most of us think we do. I also think that many folks hardly work.

My grandfather Louie DiPrisco was a fireman. I can honestly tell you I never, ever saw him actually work. I saw pictures of him in his uniform, but I never saw him put out a match, let alone a fire. So one day, in the innocence of my youth, I asked him, "Grandpa, do you ever really work?"

"*Dimbelone*," (that's Italian for *dimples*) he said, "sommatimes I worka so gosha darna hard, I no can catch my breath."

Well, I never saw Grandpa do that, but I think that's how we're supposed to work. Now how many of us actually do this?

In my career in the investment business, I have had the opportunity to interview many young people who are looking for their first job. I am always amazed when they ask me in the initial interview, "How many weeks of vacation do I get?" The Bible says, "Whatever you do, work at it with all your heart, as working for the Lord, not for men" (Col. 3:23); it doesn't say make sure you get four weeks vacation.

I think one of the most important decisions I ever made was when I chose the investment business over the shoe business. That decision allowed me to explore a passion rather than a profession. And that's the key to working hard. People ask me all the time how I can possibly work the schedule I maintain. I tell them, "I'm actually not working. To me, I'm playing golf."

What does any of this have to do with you? I'm going to suggest two things. One, whatever your problem happens to be financially, the Lord can solve it with commitment from you. And two, you can't buy the kind of passion that makes work easy. Nor can you merely say, "That sounds good. I'll try that." You will wear out. Only giving your life to Christ results in this kind of passion. Only when you recognize Jesus Christ as your Lord and Savior and he becomes your passion will you truly experience the joy of hard work.

I think that most of us have the capacity to overcome financial adversity by working harder. After all, it's a simple formula: make more money by working more hours and spend less until your debt is paid off. That is really all that is required to profit in contemporary America. The trick is in enjoying the process.

Precept 3: Train Your Children

Scripture says to, "Train up a child in the way he should go, and when he is old he will not depart from it" (Prov. 22:6 NKJV). Nothing is more important. Consider this: would you be in the financial mess you are in if someone had trained you how to handle money? My parents never taught me anything about money or how to handle it. I didn't even know how to balance a checkbook. I'll save my anger at the public school system and its inability to find a place for money management in its curriculum for another forum. The point is that the business of handling money seems to be an exercise in on-the-job-training. It's something to accomplish when you first confront it. The reality is that we need to prepare early for those kinds of decisions.

The wisdom of Proverbs 22:6 applies to the world of finance. Start with that first allowance. Explain to your children how money and the monetary system work. Most of all, teach them the ethics of work and money. Teach them that their possessions are gifts from God requiring their discipline and diligence. This conversation would be a tremendous opportunity to demonstrate the decision-making process. Take them shopping and ask them whether or not the Lord would approve of the purchase they are about to make. Does God really want your children to buy candy (or whatever it is they want)? I don't presume to know the answer, but the question should be asked, don't you think? This would be a great opportunity to gauge where your children are emotionally and spiritually.

Parents of young children should take their kids to the bank to open their first savings accounts. Children's math homework becomes an opportunity to demonstrate how to balance a checkbook. Hundreds of situations allow money to be introduced into the conversation.

Someday your children are going to buy their first home. Involve them in your discussions when you buy a home. Explain escrow, taxes, principal and interest, and private mortgage insurance. Not only does it prepare them for their own experience, it may also lead them to ask you for advice when the time comes to shop for their first house.

My point here is that children need to be trained, not lectured. Money is a lifelong reality. It can be a blessing or a curse. Wise parents will treat teaching their kids about money as an opportunity to help their children grow in their knowledge and their faith.

Precept 4: Spend Wisely

How can we spend wisely? Prayer is the answer to this one. Before you buy anything, pray about it first. This gets to the heart of the discussion on "stuff." The truth is, most people buy things because they think they deserve them. In the consumerism that engulfs America in the twenty-first century, this is called impulse buying. You walk by a display in a department store, and suddenly you simply cannot survive without a shirt from Tommy Bahama.

I wonder what would happen if, upon spying that shirt, you stopped and said, "Lord, I really like that Tommy Bahama shirt, and I think it would look good on me. But you know, Lord, it's a hundred bucks, and I'm just wondering if you think I should buy it. I'll look good in it, and by looking good, somebody may be more willing to listen to me talk about you. So, what do you think, Lord? Can I buy it?"

Now, I admit, that prayer sounds a little funky. It might, however, give you a chance to determine whether or not you actually should buy the shirt. By focusing on God's desire and not your desire, you may alter the outcome. And look at it this way—you get another chance to chat with God.

Precept 5: Practice Absolute Honesty

When I was a child, I was introduced to dishonesty, and that affected me deeply. I remember quite vividly breaking a window with a basketball when I was six years old.

My father made a claim with his insurance company. Now, in those days a claims agent actually came to your house to settle the matter. The agent asked my father, "What happened to the window?" the minute he arrived at our home. Since I was the culprit in the mishap, I was lurking in the background as the agent talked to my father.

161

I heard my father reply, "One of the neighborhood kids broke the window." Yet I had already fessed up to my dastardly act. Yes, my father lied to the agent in my presence in order to get the reimbursement.

The situation was made worse when I tried to own up to the agent. I will never forget the look of contempt on my father's face when he realized what I was trying to do. His expression said, "Shut up! Haven't you done enough already? Let me try to get out of this without it costing me an arm and a leg."

I can tell you that my relationship with my father suffered greatly from that event.

Contrast this situation with an experience recalled by James P. Lenfestey in his article "Catch of a Lifetime." Eleven-year-old James was waiting enthusiastically for the start of the bass fishing season. On the evening before the season was to begin, he was on the dock with his father, fishing for sunfish and perch.

Suddenly James's fishing pole bent way, way over. Obviously something huge had been hooked. Exhilarated, he slowly but surely reeled in his line. From the dark, murky waters he lifted the largest bass he and his father had ever seen. Both whistled and sighed in utter disbelief.

His father checked his watch. It was 10 p.m. "You'll have to put it back, son," his father said.

James thought, *But bass season is only two hours away. No one is here. No one can see what's happening. Who would know the difference?*

But James's father would not relent. He insisted that James throw the fish back into the water.

That was thirty-four years ago, Lenfestey said in his article. Never again did he come close to catching a fish like that one.[2]

But he caught something much more important that day: the importance of character and honesty, an eternal, moral lesson that shaped his life for years to come.

Solomon says it this way in Proverbs: "The integrity of the upright guides them, but the unfaithful are destroyed by their duplicity" (Prov. 11:3). And in the New Testament, Paul emphasizes this to the Ephesians: "Therefore each of you must put off falsehood and speak truthfully to his neighbor, for we are all members of one body" (Eph. 4:25).

Precept 6: Be a Generous and Joyful Giver

If you can master the concept of joyful giving, you will have won the game. An understanding of Scripture allows us to see the cycle of reciprocity that God promises. Look at Malachi 3. There God says, "Bring all the tithes into the storehouse so there will be enough food in my Temple. If you do . . . I will open the windows of heaven for you. I will pour out a blessing so great you won't have enough room to take it in! Try it! Let me prove it to you!" (Mal. 3:10 NLT).

God promises to bless us—and with a blessing so great we won't have enough room to take it in! Then he challenges us: "Try it! Let me prove it to you!" (v. 10). Nowhere else in the Bible does God challenge us like this.

My pastor, David Chadwick, teaches his congregation that the first 10 percent of their earnings belong to the Lord. And he admits that at times he and his wife, Marilynn, have been tempted to withhold their tithe to either meet an immediate need or purchase something they really wanted.

For instance, while David was in seminary, Marilynn received an invitation to go to West Virginia to be in a friend's wedding. This friend was not a Christian, and both David and Marilynn saw this invitation as an extraordinary opportunity for Marilynn to talk about how following Jesus had changed her life.

The Chadwicks checked into the plane tickets. The only way they could pay for the ticket was to use their monthly tithe, since they were only making $1,000 a month during his internship year in Houston, Texas.

They thought about the decision, they prayed, and they couldn't bring themselves to use the tithe. They felt as if they would be robbing God.

So David wrote the tithe check, and Marilynn began to compose a letter to her friend, declining the invitation.

The next day Marilynn received a letter from Southern Bell, the company she previously worked for in Atlanta. The letter stated that according to their records, Marilynn had not been paid a certain amount. A check was enclosed as the company's reimbursement.

Marilynn searched her financial records. She saw absolutely no indication of any financial payment due her. Quickly she called the phone company and protested. (She is very honest!) The company checked their records and said, yes, the money belongs to you.

She protested further.

The phone company representative assured her, "You are wrong."

But Marilynn kept protesting quite vehemently.

Finally the representative said, "Look, lady, the money is yours. Will you please take it and leave us alone?"

Marilynn felt a nudge inside her saying this was okay. Then she again checked the cost of the ticket to West Virginia. The plane ticket cost the exact amount, to the penny, of the check from Southern Bell.

When David tells this story he always reminds us that the check from Southern Bell came the day *after* he wrote the tithe check to the church.

David Chadwick is so committed to the principle of tithing that he tells the people in his twenty-plus ministry to try tithing 10 percent in faith. He says, "After one year, if God has not supplied your every need, we will restore the tithe to you in the full amount." In all the years he's taught the principle, no one has ever taken him up on the refund.

Recently I noticed another part of Malachi 3. Before God tells Israel to bring their tithes to him, he admonishes them with these words: "Should people cheat God? Yet you have cheated me! But you ask, 'What do you mean? When did we ever cheat you?' You have cheated me of the tithes and offerings due to me. You are under a curse, for your whole nation has been cheating me" (Mal. 3:8–9 NLT).

Notice that last sentence. We are under a curse if we don't give back to the Lord a part of what he has given to us. After all, as I said at the beginning of this chapter, nothing you possess is yours anyway, even the bills!

Now, God doesn't want us to give begrudgingly, just because we are afraid of this curse. He wants us to give joyfully.

If you do give to his work, here's a quick acid test to determine whether or not the check you just wrote comes from a devotion to do the Lord's work: Was it the first check you wrote after you received your paycheck? Were you excited when you wrote it? If you find yourself saying, "I'll pay it later" or "I can't afford it this month" or "I can't afford 10 percent; the Lord will understand," you might be hanging onto too much of this world.

Some people try to fool themselves. "I'll give 5 percent," they say. "Something is better than nothing." But that's not biblical. Attempting to rationalize your stewardship of the Lord's money is misreading the Bible. There's no wiggle room in Scripture. That's why I like the Bible so much.

Malachi 3 doesn't say to give some money to the Lord. Or to give 5 percent or 3 percent. God is specific: 10 percent. And he promises that when you give 10 percent of your gross income to the Lord as an offering, he will bless you.

I have a friend who rationalized her tithe. She and her husband both worked, and her husband had not grasped the significance of the tithe. Oh, they gave more than 5 percent to the Lord, but not the full 10 percent. My friend said, "Because my husband is in authority in our home, I cannot override his decision." Was she rationalizing? Probably, although I don't want to get into the theology of this dilemma.

However, when her husband retired and she was still working, she proposed that they give a full, before-tax, 10 percent tithe.

What happened next was God's blessing. All of a sudden the company her husband had worked for called and asked him to work for them as a consultant. They gave him some accounts that he had worked with over the years and told him to supervise them. And all of a sudden one of those companies received a contract for extensive fiber optic cable construction in a foreign country.

The year after they began their 10 percent tithe, my friend's husband made almost double what he had earned per year when he worked full time for the same company. That's God pouring out a blessing so great you don't have room enough to take it in!

So there it is. Now you have the formula for being a faithful steward of the Lord's possessions. Think of it this way: Imagine that you are playing on a spiritual football team. God is the head coach and the Bible is the playbook. Even without an ounce of athletic ability, you can learn to play this game. Just listen to the coach. He even wrote it down for you.

11

SHUFFLING OFF THIS MORTAL COIL

Estate Planning

I have some bad news. You are going to die. We all are. Yet to those of us who are Christians, this message delivers hope since we know where we are to spend eternity. Most people, without the benefit of belief, become uncomfortable at this news of their death. But none, short of the insane, refute it. Our death is certain.

Through various and sundry permutations of the law over the centuries in America, somehow the United States government has come to believe that they are entitled to pretty much half of what you have managed to accumulate during your lifetime. I find this unconscionable. Others do not.

Some people do not seem to mind that after their death they lose control over their assets. Their reasoning is that they are dead, so what difference does it make? If this is your attitude, skip this chapter. As a financial advisor, I believe you should care. My reasoning is grounded in having seen what transpires in families once a loved one passes. It's not always pretty. Consequently, I would like to leave clear and concise directions as to whom I want to get what when I die, and that does not include giving half of my granddaughter's legacy to the government!

Make no mistake, I am more than willing to pay those estate taxes deemed legal. The key is in not overpaying, and I plan on doing that by taking advantage of the legal processes which allow my family to inherit more of my assets. I believe you should do that as well.

The thought of paying taxes that can easily be avoided leaves me pretty cold, and I don't believe that behavior reflects good stewardship, especially if we have demonstrated our faith in our families by raising them to serve the needy in word and deed. By paying taxes we don't have to pay, we deprive our heirs of assets they can continue to use in ways that honor the Lord.

I think that the reasoning for much poor estate planning is the morbidity of the subject. Most simply don't want to think about death or dying. Estate planning is also terribly intimidating. If you have ever spent any time with an estate attorney (or any attorney for that matter), you know that talk of this marital trust or that family limited partnership or Crummy powers (believe it or not, the guy who founded this trust was named Crummy) can be just a mite intimidating.

I am not a lawyer, but I have a ton of experience working with lawyers in estate situations. So in this chapter I will attempt to eradicate some of the confusion that generally comes with the estate planning process. I'll explain in simple language some basic estate planning techniques that are available to everybody. I hope you will read carefully and then do those things necessary to keep your assets in your family for your family's benefit after you die.

What Is Estate Planning?

Estate planning is the process one goes through to specify how his or her assets should be distributed after death. Here are some of the decisions you need to consider when putting together an estate plan:

- decide how to divvy up your assets after the estate settlement costs are paid
- decide if you want to give away assets as gifts during your lifetime in order to gain a tax advantage
- choose trustees
- choose an executor or executrix
- spell out your funeral plans, organ donation, and whether or not you would like to be cremated
- choose successor custodians for minor children (if you have an account set up to benefit a minor child and you don't appoint a custodian in the event of your death, the court decides on one)
- consider charitable donations
- specify instructions on how to care for you if you become incapacitated (a living will)

These are just some of the decisions you need to make early so you won't be making these decisions on your death-bed when your mind may be muddled. I urge you to consider putting your estate plan together when you are of sound mind and body. You can make changes (codicils) when and if your life situation changes.

I urge you not to try this on your own. I can think of no situation in the world of financial planning where you have greater need for good counsel. The laws are too complex and the stakes too high to rely on your own abilities.

The Dos and Don'ts of Estate Planning

Writing a Will

This is the starting point. A will is the legal document that tells the world what you want to happen to your assets after you die. It's nothing more than that. It is not a declaration that your death is imminent. So why be afraid to write one?

Unfortunately, most folks don't realize that everybody has a written will, whether they write one or not. If you don't write one on your own and you die intestate (the intimidating legal word for not writing your own will), most states will write one for you. Here's one example of the kind of things that can happen when a state writes a will.

Let's suppose that you are married with two kids. Your wife is your second wife, and she has two kids of her own. With a will drawn by the state, half of your estate goes to your second wife with each of your children getting a quarter of the estate. Is that your intent? What if you both die at the same time in an accident? Even if your second wife's children are grown and can't handle money properly, they get half of their mother's assets. Did you really intend to leave one quarter of your estate to your second wife's ne'er-do-well children?

I guarantee you won't like the will that the state writes, and neither will your loved ones. Think about all the things up for grabs in one's lifetime besides assets. Do you want a judge to decide who gets to raise your kids? The point is that this process has far-reaching consequences and often gut-wrenching emotion tied to it. The modest amount of time and money that you devote to it is well worth the effort.

The point of a will is to allow you to retain control of your assets once you pass on. You can divide your assets *any way you like*. You can give your assets to *anyone you like*. The will covers all of your assets: houses, cars, boats. If you own it at the time of your death, you get to say who gets it. The law breaks assets into intangible assets (cash, stocks, bonds, mutual funds) and tangible assets (houses, cars, boats). For tangible personal property, insert a clause in your will outlining who gets what. Better yet, make a videotape of yourself declaring your wishes. It's hard to contest that, don't you think? In legal terminology, this is called a *tangible personal property memorandum*.

Lots of assets are handled outside of a will. For example, an IRA or pension plan where a beneficiary has been named passes outside of the will and goes directly to the beneficiary. This is true of life insurance, and if you own your home jointly with your spouse, the house goes right to this person. He or she does not have to pass go! Any property held inside a trust also goes to a beneficiary without passing through the will. This is a very important concept to remember: *assets held in a trust or placed in a trust before you die avoid probate.*

One of the most important decisions facing you will be naming an executor, the person who will be in charge of following your instructions as to how to distribute your assets after you die. Take this very, very seriously. Obviously you want an executor who is familiar with financial and legal matters. Some name a trusted family friend or an advisor like their lawyer or stockbroker to be their executor. Make sure that the executor has the power to do the job. Do not try to control things from the grave so much that you choke the executor's ability to implement your wishes.

Here's another caveat. If the person you choose is merely loved and not capable, trusted but not necessarily savvy, the estate will probably have to buy some insurance against the executor making a significant mistake. It's not cheap, so be careful. You should be guided by your head and not your heart when naming an executor. Remember, we are trying to keep as many assets as we can in the estate and not watch them melt away in the form of taxes.

When you get ready to visit your estate attorney, have some things at your disposal in order to minimize his time (they charge by the hour). Here are some of the things you should bring with you:

- a list of your tangible property (homes, cars, boats), how much you paid for them, and where they are located. Bring paperwork like deeds or anything else that will prove you own the assets. Also know how you own the assets, whether they are jointly held with your spouse or in common with somebody else.
- a list of your intangible property, like stocks and bonds. Know what you paid and when. Use your bank and brokerage statements for this, and bring them with you.
- insurance policies
- pension plans
- annuities
- bank accounts
- a list of all your debts. Do you owe money to credit card companies, banks, insurance companies, brokerage firms?
- a list of all of your advisors. Who is your banker, broker, lawyer, insurance person? How can you contact each one?

You need to remember to review your will every few years. Most people will write a will and then forget about it. Over the years I have seen many wills that don't include all of the client's children because some of them were born after the will was drawn. Too many people disinherit their children simply because they forgot to look at their will. One of the few certainties in the world of estate planning is that circumstances change. You may change careers, your net worth goes up and down, your guardians and executors may die, your parents may pass on. You need to bring your will into line with your current circumstances.

When you sign the will, make certain that it is witnessed by people who have absolutely no connection to the will. They didn't write it, nor will they benefit from it. This is important and oftentimes neglected. Remember that a will is not effective until a court validates it.

Keep several copies of your will in a safe place. I have copies of mine with my financial advisors, with my lawyer, and several in my safe at home. I gave a copy to my wife with written instructions as to what she should do should I pass on unexpectedly. I don't view this as morbid; I view this as responsible. I think my wife will probably be dazed and confused should I pass on unexpectedly, and she will need clear, precise instructions as to what to do, whom to call, and so on. I love her enough to make certain she has that information.

Nothing can erase the pain of a contested will. If your relatives are predisposed to fight over your assets after your death, no good comes of it. I urge you to make your desires known while you are still living so that no recriminations or misunderstandings as to your intent will follow your death.

The Living Will

A living will spells out your desires regarding the prolonging of your life should you be faced with a medical dilemma.

This addresses the question "Do I want them to pull the plug if there is no hope?" The living will is activated when you become physically or mentally unable to function and have no reasonable hope of returning to functionality.

The important thing to remember is that this document is separate from your last will and testament. A living will is unique and also needs to be reviewed periodically to make certain it continues to reflect your desire. Keep this document with your other medical records. I suggest you give copies to your doctor and your intended executor. At least make sure that your spouse knows where it is and what your intentions are.

In addition to the living will, you need to create a health care power of attorney document—a legal document that transfers authority to another person. This goes hand in hand with the living will since it gives someone you trust the ability to make medical decisions if you cannot.

Understanding Probate

Recognize that the vast majority of estates endure the probate process. Having a valid will makes it easier, but it is still necessary. The very first thing that the probate court does is to validate the will, so it clearly helps that you have one. Declaring the will valid means that the court believes that the will actually reflects the deceased one's desires regarding the distribution of his or her assets, and that jumpstarts the probate process.

Next the court appoints an executor. The job of an executor is to administer the estate. This is not always the easiest of tasks. I can tell you that I have counseled numerous children of deceased parents who get old while still trying to settle the estate. Usually the court just rubberstamps the person selected as the executor in the will. If the person has no will, the court appoints an executor—yet another good reason to write a will.

The court supervises the work of the executor, which includes paying the bills, distributing the assets, paying the taxes, filing the final tax return (which must be filed within nine months of the date of death if the estate is more than a minimum size determined by current tax law), and paying the legal and funeral bills. If the survivors need some money during the probate process, the executor can arrange to distribute some income and even invade some principal if necessary. The point is that being an executor is no day at the beach.

For that reason, an executor can charge a fee. The fee can either be stated in the will or set by the court. The court can even limit it as a set percentage of the total estate. Now, as a matter of good stewardship, you need to be vigilant in this area. For example, the fee can range from zero to 5 percent, or perhaps even more, of the total estate. If the will names a bank or a law firm as an executor, you need to make certain that the services rendered match the fee structure. I have seen many survivors livid because they had to pay 5 percent of an estate worth millions of dollars for relatively little work. It's best to check these arrangements ahead of time. If you hire an independent executor (not a family member), check their fee schedules. Normally, the fees go down in direct proportion to the size of the estate. Fees to settle an estate may look like this:

First $500,000	5.0%
$500–750,000	3.0%
$750,000–1.5 million	1.0%
$1.5–5 million	.5%
Over $5 million	.3%

These percentages may look benign, but do the math. Let's say that an estate worth $10 million names an independent agency like a bank as executor and the fee schedule

175

outlined above applies. The total fees collected after settling the estate would be $67,500. This may or may not be reasonable and fair compensation, depending on the work involved in settling the estate.

Keep in mind that assets in an estate can be complex. They can be stocks, bonds, and cash, but they can also be houses, boats, and even *businesses*, in addition to various personal items. The work of the executor varies with the job. Make certain that you are getting your money's worth. Obviously a family member serving as executor will probably charge far less than an independent. But remember too that any fees received as an executor are taxable income for the individual. All of the fees are, of course, paid out of the estate.

Let me warn all you potential executors out there. The job of an executor is generally a thankless one. If serving as a loved one's executor is your way of demonstrating your last full measure of devotion to the deceased, have at it. But know that the demands of the job can be stressful and frustrating and may provide a glimpse into a side of human nature that you might not really want to see. Know that the probate process could go on for a few months—or a few years! Enough said.

If the will is simple and the instructions are clear, the job may merely involve distributing the assets. But sometimes an executor may need to sell some assets in order to pay the estate taxes. Once all the assets are distributed and the taxes paid, the executor closes the estate, and the court has to approve everything that the executor did. If the court receives no challenges to the disposition of the estate, the deed is done. If you have been the executor, pour yourself a large drink of iced tea and celebrate. Your ordeal is over.

Probate proceedings are public. Some courts may even require that you post notices in newspapers regarding the sale of assets. In any event, some things that a family would like to keep private may end up public information.

As you can probably see, probate court is not a lot of fun. While it can never be avoided completely, you can minimize the effects of probate.

Minimizing Probate

Most people would like to avoid the evils of a complete probate (the judge doing more than just validating your will), but it is not easy. It takes a comprehensive understanding of estate planning and a pretty good estate attorney. You can minimize probate in four main ways:

- give away your assets while you are still alive
- title your assets properly
- use life insurance
- use trusts

Let's look at each of these suggestions.

GIFTING YOUR ASSETS

The object of this exercise is to reduce your estate's value. By doing that, you leave less for the government to tax when you die. However, it is not as easy as it sounds, except in the case of a spouse giving to a spouse. In that case, you are allowed to give away everything. You simply title everything in your spouse's name. When you die, your estate is zero and you leave no estate to tax! The problem comes upon the second death. When your spouse dies, that estate, if it's past the federal minimum, is taxed.

Some people like this scenario in that the surviving spouse gets to enjoy the maximum lifestyle until his or her death. The problem comes with the second generation. So if the issue is preserving the estate for the surviving spouse, children, and grandchildren, we need to do more planning.

Each person can give away $10,000 each year to anyone and everyone without incurring a gift tax. You and your spouse can give $20,000 to your son, your daughter-in-law, and each of the grandchildren. While the $10,000 may seem modest if you are trying to reduce a multimillion-dollar estate, it can quickly add up.

You need to be careful about giving too much away. Make certain you don't negatively impact your income by giving away so much that you have less working for you. You also need to be careful about giving gifts to people who are named in your will. Your will needs to include specific instructions that you do not want the gifts already given to be subtracted from the amount specified in your will. If you are not precise, the amount you gave to them while you were alive may be subtracted from their inheritance.

Here's another warning: large gifts given within three years of your death may be negated by the court since the court could interpret them to mean that you were giving your assets away in order to avoid the estate tax since you knew you were going to die. That's why planning early makes a lot of sense and stands up to the scrutiny of the court.

Here's a strategy that makes a great deal of sense to me. Give away assets that you think are most likely to increase in value, like a growth stock. Let's pretend that you give away 100 shares of Cisco Systems (a high-tech growth stock). It passes to your chosen one at your tax cost (what you paid for the stock). The tax only applies when that person sells the stock, presumably many years later. The stock is out of your estate, and the one receiving the gift can control when he or she wants to pay the capital gain.

Let's suppose that you bought Cisco ten years ago and this stock has highly appreciated already. You can also give Cisco to your favorite charity in exchange for an annuity, a predictable income stream. The stock gets out of your estate, the charity gets to sell it without paying capital gains tax, and you may get to take a charitable deduction. Wait, it gets better. You may even be able to set up a wealth replacement trust (a trust that replaces the money an estate has to pay for estate tax) for the amount you gifted, using life insurance, and be able to establish an income stream from it! For instance, if you figure your estate tax is going to be $500,000 (which won't happen to most of us), then you can buy life insurance with the estate of Joe Blow as the beneficiary. The estate pays the taxes but is reimbursed by the insurance payment. I'll talk more about this later on in a section dealing with how to use insurance for estate purposes.

TITLING YOUR ASSETS

The most common form of joint ownership for married couples is joint tenancy with rights of survivorship (JTWROS). When you own assets in this manner, all the assets are passed to the survivor without tax. They simply shift from the deceased to the survivor without going through probate. However, remember my warning earlier in this chapter about the taxes due upon the second death. You can own assets titled jointly with someone other than your spouse, but this is a little trickier. Be certain to check with an estate attorney before deciding to hold assets in this manner.

USING LIFE INSURANCE

Life insurance pays death benefit proceeds directly to the beneficiary without going through probate. It's the best thing about insurance, in my opinion. This provides much-needed cash to a grieving spouse. But it might be better to have some life insurance proceeds go directly into a trust, which could have been established when you were alive or could be triggered into existence with your death. I'm certain that many of us know of a situation where young children have inherited a great deal of money after a loved one died and it turned out badly. Better to have that money managed by a trustee until the minor children demonstrate some maturity or reach a certain age.

USING TRUSTS

You need to know that trusts are tricky, mainly because there are so many different types. I'm going to have to use some fancy-schmancy, five-dollar words in the following descriptions, and believe me, all this legalese makes me ill. But it's necessary, so away we go!

Inter vivos trust (during life). This is the most common technique used to avoid probate. It's a lifetime trust, meaning you set it up while you are alive to hold assets so that when you die, those assets will not be considered part of your estate. In general, only those with more than a million dollars in assets should consider living trusts. A trust sets assets aside for the eventual benefit of somebody else, and that person is the beneficiary of the trust. Sometimes the beneficiary receives income from the trust for their lifetime; then when the beneficiary passes on, the trust goes to a remainder man (a named contingent beneficiary). You can see how these things can go on for a long, long time. The principal from the trust can also be distributed. My aunt Florence set up a trust that gives income to my mother upon Florence's death and then, when my mother dies, the trust principal is disbursed to my brother and me.

Like I said, trusts are tricky deals. Three parties are involved whenever there is a trust being set up. One is the beneficiary who receives benefits—whether income or principal—from the trust. Another is the trustee, likely an independent manager, who presides over the trust, making the administrative decisions so the wishes of the grantor are fulfilled. You can name anybody as a trustee, even yourself, but I would caution that you name an experienced professional who understands fiduciary responsibility.

The third party is the lawyer. Okay, get up off the floor. It gets worse. You have to pay the lawyer! I am truly sorry. However, there is no getting around it. A trust must be established with a formal, written, legal document. You can probably do it yourself with some guidance, but this is one of those situations where getting it right is crucial to the implementation of your estate plan. So bite the bullet! Pay the piper! Just make certain he or she is worth it. One good way to find a lawyer is to ask for referrals from your financial advisor. Even though the lawyer may cost anywhere from a couple hundred dollars to a few thousand dollars, depending on the complexity of your situation, if the estate plan is done wrong, the cost to your heirs could number in the tens of thousands of dollars. Do not be penny wise and pound foolish in this regard.

Let me illustrate with a famous example. As I mentioned in chapter 2, Elvis Presley died with an estate worth about $17 million. His family ended up with less than $3 million. Enough said.

Trusts come in two basic kinds: one you can change and one you cannot. The kind you can change is called a revocable trust, and the kind that cannot be changed is called an irrevocable trust.

A revocable trust can be revoked (hence the name) or changed after it has been created. You can even cancel it altogether. Therefore, assets given to a revocable trust are not removed from a grantor's taxable estate; the government says that those assets are still under the grantor's control. With a revocable trust, you pay income taxes on any revenue generated by the trust, and estate taxes might even have to be paid on those assets remaining after your death.

This is why irrevocable trusts are kind of special. But remember, irrevocable trusts cannot be changed or cancelled once you set them up. Any assets placed into an irrevocable trust are removed from your estate permanently. You cannot get them back, so be absolutely certain of your intent. The assets leave your estate and reside in the trust. The trust becomes a separate taxable unit, which pays taxes on the income and any gains that come from the assets. That's how you avoid the taxes on the appreciation upon death. Your assets didn't grow in value; the trust's assets did.

You need to understand the purpose of a trust. Generally, you would set up either a revocable or an irrevocable trust if you were trying to take care of an incapacitated person or a minor child. Because the trust is a legal entity, you want to make certain that the assets placed in a trust for the benefit of somebody else are being handled properly. That's why a judge typically looks at the money spent out of a trust and determines if it was money well spent. That way the trustee or the guardian can't raid the cookie jar.

Trusts also allow you some measure of privacy. You can transfer your assets without telling the whole world what you are trying to accomplish. That's good, especially if you are a private person, but trusts aren't the answer to everything. For example, stock in a private business that you own probably should not go into an irrevocable trust because businesses need the flexibility to raise capital or sell assets.

As I mentioned earlier, the living trust lets you put assets into trust while you are alive. If you name yourself the trustee, you control the assets during your lifetime. But, if you become incompetent, a successor or co-trustee can take charge of the assets pretty easily since the assets are already in trust and held away from you. When you shuffle off this mortal coil, all the assets in the living trust avoid probate automatically. Living trusts save bunches of trouble and tons of money in fees and expenses.

Here's another good thing about a living trust. If you place assets in one while you are alive, your will is easier to write. You won't have that much to say if the assets are already out of your estate. Now, you probably should have a pour-over will (don't panic, that's just more fancy legal talk). A pour-over will provides for those assets that were originally left out of the trust to be distributed to the trust. A living trust is rarely contested, and that too saves acrimony and money. For example, say you place a million dollars in trust, and that takes care of the Unified Tax Credit (UTC). (Under current law, everyone is allowed to accumulate $1,000,000 free of estate tax—that is the UTC.) Then, fortunately, you live another ten years, accumulate another million dollars, and die before amending the will. The pour-over provision takes care of that next million.

A ton of unscrupulous lawyers are out holding seminars all over the country to get you to pay them thousands of dollars in fees to set up a living trust. That's bunk. Most folks, especially those with less than a million dollars in assets, do not need living trusts. You will see and hear many advertisements for free seminars touting the strategy. They may even offer you a free meal. Go, eat the meal, and remember what I told you—most likely you don't need a living trust. A will accomplishes many of the same things if your estate is modest. Save the fees and, if they are offering veal parmigiana with a side of spaghetti marinara, enjoy!

Many, many people I have counseled over the years have gone to the time and expense of setting up the living trust and then never transferred their assets into the trust. That makes no sense! Make sure you can break the hold the assets have over you by transferring the title to those assets. If you don't, simply having the trust doesn't populate the trust. All you did by creating the trust and not funding it was spend money you did not need to spend. Transferring assets is not a hard thing to do. For example, if you own assets in the Danny Fontana account, simply change the title to the Danny Fontana Trust.

Other trusts. So many different kinds of trusts exist that trying to list them all is daunting, and I really do not want to confuse you. Suffice it to say that whatever you are trying to accomplish, you can most likely find a trust that will satisfy, or at least address, your desires.

For example, let's suppose that you are married to a wonderful spouse but that this person never saw a store that he or she didn't like. You are concerned that after you pass, your money may be squandered. You want to make certain that the money lasts at least through your spouse's lifetime. A Q-TIP trust might be the answer for this dilemma.

Q-TIP stands for Qualified Terminal Interest Property, and the purpose is to control who inherits your assets after your spouse dies. A husband can establish a Q-TIP trust so the assets will go into trust upon his death. The wife cannot manage the assets or be the trustee. It must be a third party. The income generated from the trust goes to the wife for her lifetime, and she is the only person who can receive the income from the trust. But neither she nor anyone else can give away the money from the trust since the IRS has ruled that those assets cannot be shifted to someone in a lower tax bracket. The Q-TIP is a classic financial planning tool for someone in a second marriage who wants to make absolutely certain that his second wife is provided for during her lifetime but that his natural children get the money upon her death. This also keeps the wife who remarries badly from giving her money to the next husband and effectively disinheriting her children.

Many, many times people fail to consider that the proceeds from life insurance policies push their estates into higher estate tax liability. Fortunately, a life insurance trust is a way around that. These trusts are irrevocable (you cannot change them) and the death benefit from them does not go into your estate (although you have to name the proper beneficiary in order to accomplish this). The trust gets the life insurance death benefit proceeds when you die, bypassing both estate tax and probate. You can specify exactly how and when you want that money distributed.

This is a great feature if you have younger children whom you might want to get the income until they turn twenty-five years of age, at which point you want to let them have the principal. A life insurance trust also can be used to pay estate taxes. This is generally called a wealth replacement trust. I have used this technique successfully many times in my financial career to help with a huge estate tax liability.

I had a client who owned a textile company with his brother. On paper the business was worth about $30 million, making their individual estates quite large. Unfortunately, they didn't have any cash. They had a building and a business, but try paying your taxes with a loom! The solution was to buy a large insurance policy that would pay cash in an amount equal to the estate taxes. That way the surviving brother would not have to rush to sell assets or borrow the money, using the business as collateral, in order to pay the taxes. When one of the brothers died, the insurance paid off and the taxes were paid with little wear and tear on the family.

Many people want to pass assets on to charity. You can use a trust to fulfill that desire as well. A charitable remainder trust (CRT) allows individuals to give away their assets to a CRT during their lifetimes, receive the income off of the trust, and then pass the assets on to the charity after their death. This is a great way to avoid estate taxes and leave a legacy as well. The donor gets an immediate tax deduction for the contribution. Giving assets that have grown significantly makes sense since you get credit in the form of the tax deduction. In this way you avoid the capital gains tax and get the income tax deduction.

Perhaps you have started thinking about how you can link different strategies to maximize the power of your financial planning. For example, what if we used a charitable trust in tandem with a wealth replacement trust in order to save income, gift, and estate taxes and at the same time fulfill your need to be charitable? Many strategies may fit your individual circumstances. But always consult a qualified and competent advisor. In this case, use an estate attorney and an investment professional schooled in insurance before implementing these complex strategies.

Estate Taxes

Did you know that the estate tax starts at 37 percent and can go as high as 55 percent? That's right. Over half of the money accumulated during your lifetime could end up in the federal tax coffers instead of in the pockets of your heirs if you don't plan carefully. Some states even tax small estates as much as 5 percent.

For years the government allowed you to accumulate up to $600,000 free of estate tax. So a married couple could accumulate $1,200,000 that could be sheltered from tax. In recent years that amount (called the Unified Tax Credit) has gone up to $1 million each and could be headed higher. But any amount over and above the Unified Tax Credit could be taxed at very high rates indeed.

Let me illustrate the problem with the following example. First of all, you could always just leave all of your assets to your spouse with no estate tax liability. This is called the Unlimited Marital Deduction. However, if you do that, you hurt your children in the long run since you have not taken advantage of the Unified Credit Exemption (UCE). Here's what happens if someone dies with an estate of $3,000,000 and leaves it all to their spouse:

Value of estate	$3,000,000
Estate tax	0
Left to spouse	$3,000,000

Sounds like a pretty good deal—until the spouse dies. Here's what that looks like:

186

Value of estate	$3,000,000
UCE	1,000,000
Net estate	2,000,000
Estate tax	1,100,000
Left to heirs	1,900,000

Let's see what happens if we take full advantage of the Unified Credit Exemption (UCE).

Estate at first death	$3,000,000
Husband's UCE	1,000,000
Wife's UCE	1,000,000
Net estate	1,000,000
Estate tax	370,000
Left to heirs	$2,630,000

If the couple buys an insurance policy that pays a $370,000 death benefit in order to pay the taxes, the savings will be even greater!

I recognize full well the complexity of the strategies talked about in this chapter. However, I firmly believe that good stewardship demands that you take into consideration all the means available to you. If you find the task just too difficult or too many of the strategies just sound like mumbo jumbo to you, I urge you to seek competent counsel in order to fulfill the biblical mandate. I believe that good stewards want to hear our Lord say, "Well done, good and faithful servant." Effective estate planning to leave more of your assets behind in order to accomplish more of the Lord's work is part and parcel of preparing for the accolades awaiting you in heaven.

12

JOHN AND SUSIE YOUNGPERSON

A Financial Plan for Twenty- and Thirtysomethings

I can't tell you how many times people have come into my office looking for financial planning but unable to tell me what they hoped to accomplish other than to make some vague reference to "making money." I cannot stress enough to those looking for financial direction the importance of taking an inventory of their situation before approaching a planner. People need to have searched their hearts, minds, and souls in order to try to assimilate where they are and where they would like to end up. The next three chapters are designed to help you do precisely that—to walk you

189

through the financial planning process from beginning to end, from soup to nuts.

To do this, we'll look at couples in three different life situations—a young couple, a fortysomething couple, and an older couple—in the hope that the principles that apply to them will give you insight into your personal situation. You may not want to read all of these scenarios, unless you are young and want to get a feeling for the future. If you are older you may want to read the first part of this chapter and then skip to a profile that is closer to your age group. Chapter 13 describes Ben and Sally Moneymaker, a fortysomething couple, and chapter 14 portrays Bill and Vicky Elder, a retired couple.

These examples are not designed to take the place of the relationship between you and a financial advisor. I continue to urge you to forge that alliance. I don't know you, but your advisors do. I am going to make assumptions and describe fictitious people; your financial advisor deals with specific facts about your personal situation. So consider my work a guideline, a starting point, if you will.

Knowing Your Situation

Before you talk to a financial advisor, he or she will expect you to have analyzed your present situation. Photocopy the worksheet on pages 191–192 at 125 percent. Then fill out the worksheet and take it with you to the interview. I have used this worksheet for many years and have modified it as needed. Although many other companies use similar forms, I have not been able to find the original, although I have attempted to do so.

Preliminary Worksheet

Fill in the blanks below so you will be ready for the interview.

1. Are you a spender or a saver? _____
   Is your spouse a spender or saver? _____
2. Are you the beneficiary of any wills, trusts, or insurance?
   Note them here and specify the amount of each: _____
   _____
   _____
   _____
3. Are your grandparents and parents alive?
   Grandparents: _____ Parents: _____
4. If your grandparents and parents are no longer alive, how
   old were they when they died?
   Grandparents: _____ Parents: _____
5. Do you have any debt? _____ If so, how much? _____
   List credit card debt, car loans, mortgages below:
   _____ _____
   _____
   _____
6. Is your job situation stable? Yes _____ No _____
7. Where do you see yourself financially in five years?
   _____ Ten years? _____ Fifteen years?
   _____ Twenty years? _____
8. Where do you see yourself professionally in five years?
   _____ Ten years? _____ Fifteen years?
   _____ Twenty years? _____
9. When do you want to retire? _____
10. What is your current monthly income? (gross)
    _____
11. What are your monthly expenses? (To answer this question, fill in the Monthly Budget Worksheet found in the appendix.) _____
12. Are you saving any money? Yes _____ No _____ If
    so, how much per month? _____
13. Do you participate in your company's retirement program?
    Yes _____ No _____

14. How much money do you put into your company's retirement program? Husband _____ Wife _____
15. Does your company match these funds? Yes _____
    No _____ To what extent? _____
16. How do you have that money invested? (Bring a copy of your investment options with you.) _____
    _____
17. If you are self-employed, do you have an SEP IRA or similar program? Yes _____ No _____
18. How much have you put into this program? _____
19. Do you contribute the maximum allowed amount of your yearly income to this program each year?
    Yes _____ No _____
20. Do you have or need life insurance? How much?
    _____
21. If you are married, will your spouse be provided for in the event of your death? Yes _____ No _____
22. Will you inherit any money? Yes _____ No _____
    How much? _____
23. What is your net worth? (To answer this question, fill out the Net Worth Worksheet in the appendix.) _____
24. Who is your lawyer? _____
    Accountant? _____
25. How is your health? Husband: Excellent _____
    Good _____ Fair _____ Poor _____ Wife: Excellent
    _____ Good _____ Fair _____ Poor _____
26. Do you have or are you planning to have children? Yes
    _____ No _____ How many? _____ If you have children, list their names and ages: _____
    _____
27. Will you be responsible for your children's college education? Yes _____ No _____
28. Are your parents or grandparents gifting money to you now? Yes ___ No ___ If so, how much? _____
29. Please bring to the interview all paperwork you have related to money: bank statements, insurance contracts, credit card bills, student loan information, brokerage accounts, wills, trust documents, etc.

John and Susie Youngperson

Now that you have completed that preliminary assessment, let's consider the first scenario. Ready? Here we go. Meet John and Susie Youngperson, a young couple, under twenty-five years old. They are just out of college, working their first jobs, looking to buy their first home, and wanting to retire at age fifty.

John begins his comments by quickly stating their objectives. "Well, as you can see, we are a young couple just out of college, and we want some direction on how we should handle our money."

"Certainly. Let me ask you a couple of questions first," I say. "Do you have any credit card debt?"

"Yes, we do. About $4,000."

"How much does it cost you to live each month?"

"About $3,000."

"Is your income enough to cover your monthly bills, and is there any left over?"

"Yes, we can save about $500 each month."

"Okay, here's what I want you to do. Pay off the credit card debt, save three to six months of living expenses, and leave that in cash in a money market account. Then come back to see me. You are not ready to embark on an investment strategy until you meet those two criteria. Okay? Get rid of the debt, have $9,000 to $15,000 in cash in a money market account for emergencies, and then come back to see me."

This interview was short and sweet. But those two foundational elements are at the core of any savings plan. First, you must be rid of *all* credit card debt because the interest rates will eat your cash flow alive, and second, you must have an emergency reserve fund in case life throws you a curveball. You never want to be in the position where you need to sell assets in order to meet an unplanned need. That is the quickest way I know to destroy a carefully crafted investment strategy.

You need to notice that I am *not* suggesting that this young couple have no debt before starting to save and invest. Obviously they may have a car payment, a college loan, or a home mortgage. Those items represent parts of the investment strategy: How do we pay off the car loans and the college liability? The point is that while this couple is not ready to invest because of the credit card debt and the lack of an emergency reserve, they may be ready once those items are attended to, even if they have other debt.

John and Susie Youngperson return after they have paid off the credit cards and established a sufficient emergency reserve. I begin another interview:

"How old are you folks?"

"I'm twenty-five and Susie is twenty-three," John says.

"Plan on having any children?"

"Sure, but probably down the road a little bit. We want to get a little more established first. Maybe buy a house."

"Great. Do you both work?"

"Yes, I'm a planning engineer with the city, and my wife is a teacher."

"How much money are you making?"

"I make $33,000 and she is making $22,000. Together we gross $55,000."

"How much do you take home after tax?"

"About $3,300 per month."

"What does it cost you to live?"

"Maybe $2,500."

"Okay, we need to eliminate the maybe. Let me ask my question this way: at the end of the month, after the bills are paid, is there any money left over?"

"Very little."

"Well, then you must be spending more than $2,500, don't you think? If you are taking home $3,300 and there is nothing left, you must be spending it. . . . Here's a better question. Do you think you could actually live on $2,500 each month with some effort?"

"Yeah, I think so."

"Okay, now, are you spenders or savers?"

"Well, I think we are both savers." Susie nods her head in agreement.

"That works. So, first thing, make a budget to live on $2,500 and save $800 each month. Do you think that can be done?"

"Absolutely."

"Okay, then let's start by establishing a goal of saving $500 each month. That leaves you $300 of miscellaneous money to go out to dinner and so on. . . . Now, let's talk about your health history. Are your parents alive?"

"Yes, both sets of parents are alive."

"What about your grandparents? What I am trying to get at is whether or not there is any history of disease like cancer or heart attacks in your families."

"One of my grandfathers died of lung cancer at sixty-two, and one of my grandmothers had a heart attack at seventy-seven," John says.

"All four of mine are alive," Susie adds.

"Do either of you smoke?"

"No."

"Have you prepared wills?"

"No."

"Well, that's one of the first things we have to do. What's your net worth?"

"Well, we don't have much, not even a house yet, but I would guess that we have about $50,000 worth of stuff."

"How much of that is liquid? How much is in stocks and bonds that can be readily turned into cash?"

"About half of that—maybe $20,000 to $25,000. My Aunt Minnie died and left us most of that."

"With the ability to save $500 a month, you guys can finish really strong. What about your parents? Do you expect to inherit any money or be the beneficiaries of any trusts?"

"Yes, my parents and my wife's parents have done really well. I don't know about the amount of any inheritance, but I suspect it might be substantial. They are young, though, so it will be a very long time before we see any of that money. Besides, we are self-sufficient, both have good jobs, and would like to plan without taking that into consideration."

"That's fine. I admire your self-sufficiency, but we need to factor in some money that may or may not come from them. For example, if you have kids, would their grandparents want to help fund their college educations? Or maybe they might want to reduce their estates by gifting money to you guys each year. Anyway, it's something we need to keep in the back of our minds. What about life insurance?"

"I think I have some at work."

"I do also," his wife replies.

"What's the face amount of the policies, and what kind of insurance is it? Is it term or whole life? For now we can presume that if it is from your work, it's a small amount and it's term. John, have you given any thought to how your wife will survive if anything happens to you unexpectedly? I mean, can your wife live on just her salary?"

"Probably not."

"Well, then we need to consider buying enough term life insurance to protect her in case something happens to you. You are young, so the premiums will be affordable. There goes part of those 300 miscellaneous dollars."

"What about buying insurance on my wife?"

"Well, will you need to replace her income, or can you live comfortably on your salary?"

"I think I'd be okay."

"Well, we can look at it, but it's probably not a high priority. Of course, when children enter the equation, that priority gets a lot higher. What about the house you mentioned? When do you want to look into buying your first house, and how much do you want to spend?"

"We were thinking that before we're thirty years old, we would like to be in a house and have it be nice—maybe cost $150,000 to $175,000."

"Okay, let's make that one of the lynchpins of our strategy. You want to own a house within five years. That means you are going to need at least $35,000 for a 20 percent down payment on a $175,000 house. By putting down 20 percent, you save paying the private mortgage insurance, and that can be significant. Also, by saving $500 a month and already having $25,000 in liquid investments, you won't have to go very long before accomplishing that goal. But it sounds to me like that is priority number one. Is that right?"

"Yeah, we think so, but why does that matter?"

"If you want to own a home within five years, you are going to have to save aggressively and invest conservatively. We will set aside money in cash and make sure that we can't lose any of it because the time frame, only five years, is so short. You won't make much money on those short-term investments since we will have to use fixed income investments, like a money market or short-term certificates of deposit, to achieve the goal. But you will have the house for a long time." (Obviously, many young people don't have an inheritance from an Aunt Minnie, so they will have to wait longer to purchase a house and pay less for it.)

"Okay, we have taken care of the first priority, buying a house. Now, what else is important to you?"

"Retirement. I want to retire when I'm fifty. You think that's possible?"

"Anything is possible, but let me just say that not many people really do that, and the reason is not really financial. As you get older and have kids, your priorities change. It might be possible to do that if you got raises each and every year and never had children. But you want to have children. That generally means a bigger house, more mouths to feed, paying for college. It's also possible that as you approach fifty, you won't want to retire. But that's a long way off.

We can run the numbers to see, but for right now, I would suggest that we evaluate your financial situation every year to account for any changes.

"What about your jobs? How stable is your employment and where do you see yourselves in five years?"

"I will probably still be working for the city for more money or maybe for another city. And my wife's job is portable, so job wise I think we're okay."

"You both like what you do for a living?"

"Yes."

"At work, do you participate in your companies' pension plans, 401(k) or 403(b), anything like that?"

"Yes, both of us do. My wife contributes 3 percent of her salary and I save 2 percent of mine."

"Do the companies make matching contributions?"

"Yes, I think it's half of what we put in, but it varies from year to year."

"If buying a house is your primary goal, we'll focus our initial savings efforts there. But the next thing we want to do is to increase your contributions to the pension plans, especially if they are pre-tax dollars. You will never see the money so you can't blow it, you will get a tax break, and the money will grow tax deferred, so make a note to increase your contribution as soon as you can."

"Will you help us with how we invest that money?"

"Sure, that's one of the things I can do. Get me a list of your investment choices, and we will look up the investment performance of those funds. Then I'll recommend what funds you should invest in and the percentage amounts that go into each fund."

"That's great, thanks."

"Let me try to sum up your situation and give you some idea of what we need to work on: You are young and married with no children. You have no will. Your jobs are stable. You want to buy a house within five years in the $150,000–$175,000 price range. You have $25,000 already saved in liquid investments.

You would like to have children. You would like to retire at fifty. You do not have enough life insurance. You can save $500 each month. You are healthy, with a decent family health history. You are participating in a retirement program at work but minimally. You might inherit a considerable amount of money some day. You have no credit card or installment debt. You apparently have no budget or savings plan in place.

"Is my analysis of your situation correct, or is there something else I should know?"

"No, I think that's about it. What do we do now?"

"For right now, nothing. We are going to need some time to formulate a game plan for you. I will need you to give me a worksheet showing me your income and your monthly expenses. Paychecks will help. Then go through your checkbook to see how you are spending your money. Also, I will need a net worth statement showing me everything that you own and everything that you owe. If you will do that for me, I can get cracking on your financial plan. How about making another appointment in a week or so? Then we will have a financial plan for you."

The above scenario is pretty indicative of how a first interview would go. The young couple's situation is not that complex, so the interview did not have to reinvent the wheel. Here's a snapshot of the Youngpersons' net worth statement and monthly budget.

Net Worth Statement

Assets

Cash	$2,000
Mutual Funds	10,000
Savings Bonds	8,000
401(k) for John	3,000
403(b) for Susie	1,000
Autos	20,000
Total Assets	$44,000

Liabilities

Car Loans	$15,000
Total Liabilities	$15,000

Net Worth (assets minus liabilities)	$29,000

Monthly Income and Expenses

Income

John's Salary	$2,750
Susie's Salary	1,833
Total Income	$4,583

Expenses

Income Tax (28 %)	$1,283
Rent	1,000
Food	400
Car Payments	75
Phone	50
Cable	50
Utilities	100
Entertainment	200
Clothing	100
Miscellaneous	500
Total Expenses	$3,758
Potential Savings	$825

With just a quick glance at these documents, a couple of facts stick out. First of all, we can see that this young couple is spending a good deal of money on the ever-popular "miscellaneous" category, yet they still should have $825 left over for investment. However, in the interview they said they had very little left over for investment. So where is the money really going? That's the $64,000 question. And that is why I recommend that all my clients keep track of their monthly cash outlays in addition to tracking their checkbook expenses. That gives them a better handle on how their money is being spent—or perhaps wasted.

The question I would ask is whether or not John and Susie Youngperson are spending a pretty good amount of money on vacations. Most young people with discretionary dollars find living the good life easy to do. In any event, the budget reveals an opportunity for this couple to save even more than their interview suggested. If we can get them focused, they could acquire the house even faster than they indicated. Maybe we could motivate them to trade the fancy, short-term vacations for the long-term stability of a home.

The next thing I noticed is that they have a pretty good leg up on a down payment on their house. Let's assume that they found a house for $175,000. They have enough in mutual funds and savings bonds (assuming they have matured) to put down a 10 percent deposit. I would make them aware of that situation and give them the choice. Of course, we always have to keep in mind that if they choose that solution, their emergency reserve will be depleted, so they would have to replace that. But I would also point out that a home is likely to appreciate more rapidly in price than money in a cash account at the present interest rates. My advice here would be to start looking for that house with the caveat that the money they save monthly needs to go toward replenishing their cash reserves.

I also would make the case that the money the Youngpersons are currently paying in rent ($1,000) comes pretty close to what their monthly mortgage payment would be. Say they took a mortgage of $157,500 on a $175,000 house with a down payment of $17,500 at 5.5 percent interest for thirty years. Their payment would be $856 without taxes and insurance. Again, I would give them the choice, but the opportunity to buy the house sooner rather than later starts to become compelling since the factors that favor home ownership versus renting are significant. With home ownership you get the appreciation and the tax write-off of the mortgage interest. You get neither from renting.

The next issue to address is the Youngpersons' investment strategy. Clearly, given the ages of the clients, we need to use a growth strategy. So, relying upon our investment triangle (see page 28), we would want to structure a 90/10 scenario. That's where we keep 10 percent of our investment dollars in dead, flat, safe investments like a money market or a short-term certificate of deposit and expose the other 90 percent to the stock market in a disciplined, diversified posture. Of that 90 percent, we might put 30 percent in large cap growth stocks, 20 percent in large cap value stocks, 25 percent in mid cap value stocks, 10 percent in small cap value stocks, and 15 percent in a diversified international portfolio of stocks. Of course, the vehicle of choice would be mutual funds, since they have a limited amount of money available for investment and mutual funds provide the best opportunity for diversification.

The above thoughts are the back-of-the-envelope process I use as a first attempt at my final recommendations. Of course, the written plan would address all of the necessary areas one by one and would look something like what follows.

FINANCIAL PLAN OF JOHN AND SUSIE YOUNGPERSON
Prepared by Danny Fontana

GOALS

1. To purchase a home within the next five years
2. To have children
3. To write a will
4. To retire by age fifty
5. To create a budget
6. To remain free of unsecured debt

7. To have investments that outpace inflation
8. To have an income upon retirement from investment without impacting principal

Next the plan would feature their net worth and income statements. Since we have already seen those, I will not repeat them here. The next step would involve the recommendations.

Home Ownership

Clients currently have the resources to purchase a home in the $150,000 to $175,000 price range. We recommend that they seriously consider proceeding in this direction and would be glad to offer suggestions as to realtors and mortgage companies to assist in the effort.

Debt

Clients currently have insignificant debt and are free of all credit card debt. We strongly recommend that they maintain this posture, look to pay off their car loans, and, once they purchase a home, utilize a home equity line of credit.

Estate Planning

At present, the clients have no written will. Our recommendation is that they have one executed as soon as possible. They have no estate taxation issue at present; therefore, they do not need anything complex. Simple wills that establish the clients' desires are probably all that is necessary, although we do recommend owning and titling their assets in joint name with rights of survivorship. We also recommend establishing a living will and durable power of attorney for health care in which clients express their desires should incapacitation result during their lifetimes. These documents can be accomplished through software readily available, although we believe the use of an attorney would be appropriate.

Life Insurance

John does not have enough life insurance. We recommend a term life insurance policy naming Susie as beneficiary in an amount sufficient to replace John's income in the event of tragedy. Further, we recommend that disability insurance also be purchased in addition to that which John may or may not currently have through his employer. Typically, the amount provided at one's work is not enough. The term life insurance can be purchased inexpensively and locked in for a set period of time.

We would recommend that John purchase $500,000 of term life insurance with a ten-year term certain premium. Given the clients' ages, this can be accomplished quite frugally. Should children enter the picture, we would probably need to increase the amount of insurance. We are of the opinion that, given John's age and lifestyle, life insurance is not needed on Susie at this time other than the normal coverage provided by her employer; however, disability insurance should be explored. We will be glad to provide quotes and referrals for this type of coverage.

Retirement Planning

The desire to retire at fifty is ambitious, especially if children are a consideration. However, since John is twenty-five, this is not impossible. Clients will have to be aggressive in their savings habits. The important goal is establishing cash flow that tracks the rate of inflation in order to provide an income in their retirement years that does not deplete their investment portfolios. We further anticipate that John and Susie, given their family health history, will probably reach at least eighty years of age, so they must plan to fund a lifestyle without the benefit of a paycheck for thirty years after retirement.

John and Susie are currently taking home almost $3,300 monthly after tax. In twenty-five years, it will take $9,600 (at a 3 percent inflation factor) to maintain that level of income. In order to accomplish an income from their investments that guarantees they will not deplete the principal, and assuming a yield on those investments of 5 percent, they would need to accumulate approximately $2,350,000.

Assuming that they start with their liquid investments after purchasing their first home for $175,000, save a minimum of $6,000 each year ($500 per month) for 25 years as part of their monthly budget program, and also save $5,500 per year in individual retirement plans at work that earn 9 percent, John and Susie will have accumulated approximately $1,117,776. This is a shortfall of $1,232,224.

This dilemma does have solutions. Although financial planning is not an exact science, we can make certain presumptions. John and Susie will earn more than their present salaries. As a result, their savings dollars in both programs will go up even if their percentages remain the same. This good news is offset by the variables of living. They may have children. They may have more children than they planned for. These kids may choose Harvard instead of a state university. The point is, that to reach their stated goals, John and Susie will need to earn more and spend less in order to save more.

We also can tweak their asset allocation in order to bump up their total return. For example, if we assume they earn 10 percent on the aforementioned scenario, the end result is $1,314,516. If we assume 12 percent, the result is $1,827,841. In order to obtain those results, we would have to expose their portfolio to a more aggressive risk posture. However, we do not recommend this strategy at this time. We would prefer getting to know their ability to tolerate risk before we embark on a strategy that entails more risk than overall market averages.

The stock market will be the vehicle of choice given the need to earn a minimum rate of return of 9 percent. We anticipate a 90/10 split of their invested assets: 90 percent growth vehicles and 10 percent fixed income investments. We will utilize mutual funds for the growth piece of the portfolio with the following breakdown:

30% large cap growth stocks
20% large cap value stocks
25% mid cap growth and value stocks
10% small cap stocks
15% international stocks

For the fixed income portion of the portfolio, we will utilize a money market and short-term certificates of deposit as yield opportunities present themselves.

The critical part of John and Susie's investment portfolio is not the assets they currently hold. The success of this financial plan will depend solely on the monthly contributions that they make and the consistency of those contributions. Therefore, we strongly recommend that their investments into the mutual funds be set up on an automatic basis. The mutual funds will draft their checking account each month for the amount of the investment. In this way, dollar cost averaging will assist in accomplishing a more favorable rate of return and smooth out any bumps in the stock market road. Additionally, once we reach certain break points, lower commissions will apply to those purchases.

John and Susie also need to be mindful of any inheritances, windfalls, tax refunds, and bonuses that come their way and not view those as spending opportunities. Careful budgeting will eliminate or help to minimize impulse purchases.

Annual Review

We will meet with John and Susie on an annual basis to determine whether or not our planning remains on track. Of course, should they need to meet with us more frequently, we remain at their disposal. We look forward to this opportunity to help them attain their financial goals, and we offer our gratitude for their confidence.

Let me add a note of caution for young people just starting out. If you have just graduated from college, you may be experiencing for the first time the joys of paying back college loans or overextended credit cards. You should take from those experiences the importance of limiting your use of credit. Unsecured debt (debt for which there is no collateral) is the enemy of all financial planning strategies. Debt is to be loathed. Consider that making minimum payments on a credit card debt of $5,000 at 18 percent interest requires over thirty years to pay it off. *Thirty years!* Here's the secret: pay off your debts as soon as you can. Remember the first thing I told the young people who came to see me: have no debt and have three to six months of living expenses in liquid, available funds at all times before ever starting an investment program.

13

BEN AND SALLY MONEYMAKER

A Sample Plan for the Fortysomething Age Group

Most of you who purchased this book have probably been working for a few years and have suffered some of the slings and arrows that life has to offer. You might even have a couple of children in college or looking to start. You have a job, a pension, and responsibilities, and it all just might seem a tad overwhelming at times. Well, fasten your safety belt. Hopefully, this chapter will smooth out some of those bumps for you.

Ben Moneymaker is a fortysomething, mid-level executive. He and his wife, Sally, have two children, ages fifteen and seventeen. Ben has worked as a manager in a large corporation for twenty years. He wants to retire at age sixty-five, put his children through college, travel after retirement, and maybe purchase a second home at the beach.

For their interview Ben and Sally bring their wills, power of attorney documents, insurance contracts, brokerage statements, bank statements, 401(k) statements, pension plan documents, stock option exercise papers, net worth statement, list of monthly expenses, income figures, last year's tax return, custodial accounts for minor children, and trust documents—anything and everything relating to their financial affairs.

This couple filled out the Preliminary Worksheet in chapter 12 before the interview. Clearly, their situation is going to be more complex than the Youngpersons', given their age and circumstances. Once again, this scenario is not meant to mirror your circumstances. I have given Ben and Sally Moneymaker a lot of assets so you can see all the areas that can be improved by a good financial plan. The advice will apply only to this couple. However, you can glean the principles that apply to your personal circumstances in order to formulate a basic plan of attack.

Ben and Sally Moneymaker

Ben Moneymaker began our interview by explaining their circumstances. "I have always been able to make money, but it seems that we don't have any. Our children are getting ready to go to college, and we're worried about that. Also, I'm not getting any younger, and my 401(k) got hammered last year. I'd like to do a better job at managing our money. I've realized that I am not good at it and need a professional's advice. That's why we came to you."

"Well, thanks, I appreciate the opportunity. Before we get into any specifics, let me explain exactly how this process works. First, this is a process. Today we are going to spend a fair amount of time getting to know you, Sally, and the kids. We are going to try to find out what makes you happy and miserable. Then we are going to try to uncover all of your financial issues. In order to offer solutions, we have to know the problems. Then, after a suitable amount of time spent researching what we need to recommend to you in order to solve your financial issues, we will call you back for a second appointment. Sound good?"

"Sounds fine."

"Great. Now I have to ask you a few thousand nosy questions. Okay?"

"Fire away."

"How old are you folks?"

"I'm forty-four and my wife is forty-five."

"What are your children's names and ages?"

"Justin is seventeen and Molly is fifteen."

"Are you going to pay for their college education?"

"Yes."

"Have you set aside any money for that?"

"Not really. Our parents have indicated some willingness to help with their schooling."

"Are your parents in a position to assist in any meaningful way?"

"I think so."

"Have you talked to them about that possibility?"

"Not yet, no, but we intend to do that."

"Are both sets of parents alive and healthy?"

"Yes. They are all in their mid-to late sixties and have no major health problems."

"What about your grandparents? How long did they live?"

"My grandparents on my father's side lived into their eighties. My mother's side made it to their late seventies."

Sally added, "My grandparents are still alive and in their eighties—all but my grandfather on my father's side, who died of cancer in his early sixties."

"Did he smoke?"

"Yes."

"Do either of you?"

Both Ben and Sally quickly answer no.

"Okay, let's move on to your job situation. Where do you work, what do you do, and what do they pay you for that?"

"I'm a senior vice president with a Fortune 500 corporation, and I run a division that employs sixty-five people. My base salary is $125,000 plus a bonus based on profitability. Last year my bonus was $50,000."

"That's terrific, good for you! What about you, Sally? Do you work?"

"Yes, I'm a computer programmer. I make about $50,000."

"So you guys have a very handsome income."

"Yes," Ben admits. "But I can't figure out why we don't have any money."

"Are you spenders?"

"We live well."

"So you are?"

"I guess you could say that. We have a home on a golf course, drive nice cars, and eat out a lot. We also take very nice vacations every year."

"Tell me about your house. Do you have a mortgage and if so, how much do you owe?"

"Well, we bought it for $1,000,000 and put $150,000 down. The mortgage is about $850,000."

"What is the interest rate on the mortgage?"

"I think we're paying like 6½ percent, something like that."

"Let's find that out exactly; we may be able to refinance at a lower rate and save some major dollars. Do you think that your job situation is stable? Any chance you could get fired without much notice?"

"You never really know, but I've been there a good long time, so I think I'm okay."

"As a senior vice president, have you been granted any company stock options?"

"Yeah, quite a few, but I never follow that closely. I brought a document with me that explains all of that."

"Great, we'll need that. Do you know what you paid for the options, if anything?"

"I don't know. I think I'm involved with the company stock through a payroll deduction, and there's a deferred compensation program as well. Like I say, I've got all that stuff, and I hope you'll look at it."

"Of course." I am not surprised that Ben knows so little about his company plans and his financial situation. Some people like Ben are so busy making money and spending it that they don't take time to keep track of their financial assets. Still, I prod him further. "Do you think you have significant dollars invested in the options and the deferred comp?"

"I think so. I get more every year if the company and my division do well. So, yeah, I would say so."

"Well, this is an area where we have to spend a pretty good amount of time. We'll probably have more questions for you as well. Do you have a 401(k)?"

"Yes, and I brought that statement with me. I think I've got like $350,000 in it."

"How is it invested?"

"I'm not exactly sure. I know it's in mutual funds, but I can't tell you which ones or how much is in them. As you can see, I'm not very detail oriented about this stuff. That's why we came to you guys."

"Okay, we'll look at that as well. . . . All right, let's get to some tougher questions. How much does it cost you each month to live?"

"Shoot, I don't have a clue. Probably $10,000 to $12,000?"

"It's got to be more than that. Your mortgage at 6.5 percent on $850,000 is going to be somewhere around $5,000. Are the kids in private school?"

"Yes, I forgot about that. The tuition is pretty steep too. For both of them, it's like $15,000 a year total."

"Well, there's another $1,250 a month. We haven't even broken a sweat, and we're at $6,250 a month. We are going to have to take a detailed look at your spending patterns. I need you to go through your checkbooks and list all your fixed expenses. Break down anything that's discretionary, like clothing or entertainment, and label it in a 'miscellaneous' category. My guess is that you guys are inadvertently spending a ton of money that we can target for savings. Do you have any outstanding balances on credit cards?"

"Yeah, but not much. Something like $10,000."

"*Te salute,* Don Corleone."

"What do you mean?"

"If you think that $10,000 on a credit card isn't much, you have too much money. Seriously, we need to pay that off. By carrying such a large balance you are literally giving money to the credit card company. Trust me, they have enough money. Let's redirect some of that into a college program for the kids."

"I know you're right. It's just convenient to charge stuff."

"I know, but we need to inject some discipline into your plan. Getting rid of credit card debt is a basic fundamental of all financial planning. Debt's not a good thing, especially 18 percent debt."

"Okay, I hear you."

"Good, let's move on. When do you plan on retiring, or are you going to work forever?"

"Well, I really like working. My guess is that I'll retire at sixty-five and then do volunteer work of some kind."

"What about you, Sally? Do you want to retire?"

"I'd like to retire when Ben does, and then we could spend time at a beach house or travel the world."

"Well, it's certainly possible, but first we have to get a handle on your spending. . . . You mentioned a beach house. Is that something you aspire to?"

214

"Yes, Ben and I both love the beach. Actually, we would like to get a place now if we could."

"Well, let's see if you can afford it. Let's get into your portfolios. What's your net worth, Ben?"

"I guess it's a little over a million."

"Okay, you have $150,000 worth of equity in the house and $350,000 in the 401(k). What else do you have?"

"I have a little over $100,000 in a brokerage account at XYZ Brokerage. I brought that statement for you as well. I've lost a bunch of money in that account. It used to be worth about $250,000."

"You're kidding."

"No. I got caught up in that high-tech stuff back in the late nineties and lost my shirt. That's what got Sally's attention, and she insisted that I talk to a professional."

"Let me take a quick glance at the statement. . . . I see what you mean. This is aggressive as heck. That's the bad news. The good news is that we can probably get some decent tax losses when we sell out of this stuff."

"Would you sell it? Don't you think we ought to wait until the price rebounds a little bit?"

"And when might that be?"

"I don't have a clue."

"That's the point. It can also go down farther, can't it? The question is whether or not the investments in your portfolio match your ability to stomach the losses. You may be able to, but you just said that Sally is nervous. It's her money too, isn't it? Anyway, let's test your risk profile. Are you game?"

"Sure."

"Let's pretend that you gave me $100,000 to invest six months ago, and you opened your statement and saw that, on paper, it was worth $95,000. How would you feel?"

"I'm okay with that." (True statement. I'm watching for a flinch.)

"Okay, what if it were $85,000?"

There's a slight hesitation before Ben answers, "I'm okay with that."

"I can tell that you are not. What we just discovered is that your risk tolerance is about 10 to 15 to maybe even 20 percent in a year, but then it bothers you. This is a very important distinction, because we now know to limit your exposure to loss to less than 20 percent in any given year. We will be able to do that by the proper investment mix called asset allocation. We then have to match that investment profile to your goals to see if they are achievable. We'll present that to you at our next meeting. I'm also going to need that net worth statement since I suspect you aren't quite worth what you think you're worth. List everything you own and everything you owe, and the difference is your net worth. Okay?"

"Sure, I'll get it to you as soon as I can. What about insurance? Do you think that I need it?"

"How much do you have?"

"I think I've got like a half a million with the company, but I'm not sure."

"Well, this is an issue to consider. Should something happen to you, your wife would be saddled with huge obligations. We need to determine whether or not there would be enough money to bury you, pay off the mortgage, educate the kids, and let her live comfortably for the rest of her life. Being pretty young, you ought to be able to skin this cat with some inexpensive term insurance."

"Will you do that?"

"We'll shop for you and try to get the best deal we can, but we probably won't write the policy ourselves. I need to tell you that you have some formidable issues facing you in the future. Fortunately, you have an impressive net worth given your age, and your income is certainly impressive. However, it is clear that you are not very astute financially. For that reason, we have to talk about how we work with a client.

"Now, I do not mean to offend you, but the one thing we are going to have to address is whether or not you are comfortable taking our recommendations. Quite frankly, it bothers me that you tried to pick stocks. I'm worried that you might want to do that again, especially if the stock market heats up. You lost a bunch of money because you did not know how to pick stocks. Because of that, you increased your risk profile significantly without even knowing it. The stakes going forward are too high.

"I'm also worried about financing college for the kids. If you try to pay for it out of current cash flow, as you may have to, your lifestyle will suffer for a few years. But we'll address that, factoring in any gifts you might receive from your parents. We'll probably look at a 529 plan for Molly, your younger child. I just don't think there is much we can do for Justin, your older child. So we have some work to do. Are you comfortable with all of this?"

"Well, I would like to hold onto a few dollars in order to trade some stocks. I enjoy that."

"It's your money. But if you are going to ask me what I think of such-and-such a stock at such-and-such a time, I won't be very helpful. I'm telling you on the front end, that's not what we do. As a professional, I know that trying to pick stocks on a timing basis doesn't work. I am also recommending that you stay out of it. But it's your money. How much cash do you have in checking or savings accounts?"

"Not very much—maybe $5,000 in a money market at the bank."

"That's not enough. We're going to have to beef that up. You should have at least three to six months of cash, just in case of an emergency. Do you have written wills?"

"Yeah, but they were written years ago in a different state. I think they were even written before we had our second child; she's fifteen, so you can see how old they are."

"We have to make that a priority. If you walk out of this office and get hit by a bus on the way to your car, your kids have a huge problem. Do you have a relationship with an estate attorney?"

"No . . . can you recommend one?"

"Sure, but first we really need to look at your financial situation in its entirety so that we can get some idea of the complexity of your estate. Then we'll know who to recommend."

"An estate attorney is expensive, right?"

"Best bang for the buck you will ever get if it's done right. I suspect your issues will have more to do with how you have things titled than with burdensome estate taxes, but an attorney can be quite helpful with all of that. What about other assets besides what you have shown me? Do you have any other real estate? Collectibles?"

"Yes, we own some rental properties around town."

"Oh, okay. How many, and do they have positive cash flow?"

"We have small mortgages on two, and one is paid in full."

"How much do you owe on the mortgages?"

"For both of them, probably about $100,000."

"Let me ask it this way: how much are the mortgage payments?"

"One is $650 and the other is about $600."

"So in total $1,250. How much is the rent?"

"We collect about $2,100 each month."

"Is it reliable?"

"Yes, all of our tenants have been there for a while now."

"Okay. So you owe $100,000 on two properties, and one is free and clear. What are they worth if you were to sell them?"

"I'd guess maybe $350,000."

"Great! We've got a quarter of a million dollars' worth of equity that we can lean on if we have to. What are your plans for these properties? And do you intend to acquire any more?"

"I don't really know. I guess we always thought of the properties as a safety net of sorts, our retirement contingency fund."

"So that's where the idea of the beach house comes from. You might think about selling a house or two when you retire so you can buy a house at the beach and kick back. What would you do with the house you live in now?"

"Again, I'm not certain that we know. Do we need to know that now?"

"No, but it is something to think about. One of the basic tenets of financial planning is to have no outstanding mortgage at the point of retirement. Here's the consideration: if your house has no mortgage when you retire twenty years from now and it's worth a million dollars today, you may have another couple million dollars of equity staring you in the face at retirement. You could sell your primary residence for a couple million dollars and pay cash for a retirement home at the beach. That might be a very attractive scenario for you. Would that be something you would like to see on paper?"

"Sure, we'd have to consider that, wouldn't we."

"I think you would. And we need to consider another scenario as well. Obviously, you may have the capability of funding various charitable and civic projects if that's your desire. A charitable remainder trust might be something you want to consider."

"We are givers. We tithe to our church, so that is something we would be interested in exploring."

"Okay, well, you have given us a ton of things to think about. Let us get through your documents, put a preliminary process together, and then try to get specific about our recommendations."

Ben Moneymaker might seem to be an exaggeration because he has so little knowledge of his financial affairs.

Through much experience in financial planning I not only know that smart people do dumb things with money all the time, I would suggest that it is the rule rather than the exception. Just because people are good at their jobs doesn't mean they are good at managing money. In fact, quite often the opposite is true.

A Financial Analysis

As you can readily see by contrasting this couple with our first couple, the Moneymakers' situation is much more complex. Let's start with their combined income and cash flow statement.

Monthly Income and Expenses

Income

Ben's Salary	$10,500
Sally's Salary	4,167
Total Wages	14,667
Federal Tax	5,573
State Tax	1,027
FICA	1,122
Total Taxes	7,722
Net Wages Monthly	$6,945
Rental Income	2,100
Total Monthly Income	9,045

Expenses

Mortgages	
Primary	5,500
Rentals	1,250
Tuition	1,250

Utilities	500
Phones	150
Cable	200
Tithe	1,458
Cars	1,530
Food	1,000
Entertainment	500
Clothing	500
Miscellaneous	500
Total Expense	$14,338
Shortfall	<5,293>

It's clear that these folks are living way over their heads, and it becomes easy to understand why they have a home equity line of credit. Without the $50,000 bonus payment from Ben's company each year (which is not included in the monthly income statement), the Moneymakers would be heading down a path of debt-induced misery. The monthly deficit in their cash flow is tantamount to an open hemorrhage, and the flow of blood must be stopped.

I must tell you that in over twenty years of dispensing financial advice I have seen that the propensity to spend more money than earned is the most common malady affecting people who inadvertently have made money their god. I don't think there is any mistaking where the Moneymakers' heart truly is. Even though they have a willingness to give to the church, I don't think it a stretch to presume that they are into "thangs"—the stuff of this world.

My point is that the Moneymakers should not be dismissed as far from typical. Indeed, my experience proves that they are typical, though perhaps not in how much money they make at such a young age. That is clearly rather unusual. What is typical is their need to buy things they cannot afford in order to fill the holes in their heart. If you listen to their goals and aspirations, you do not hear

221

"feed the hungry, heal the sick, and give more to worthy causes." What you hear is, "retire early, buy a beach house, drive expensive cars, and travel the world." Even though they said they are givers, I see little evidence of this in our discussion.

Most financial advisors would not mention this to the Moneymakers. Most would simply invest the money for them and make the commission and the financial planning fee. Since the Moneymakers are professing Christians, I would feel compelled to talk with them about their spiritual situation to try to determine exactly what might be missing in their lives that makes them feel the need to spend money they don't have.

My financial plan will reveal the problem and then also offer financial solutions. Fortunately, the Moneymakers do have a handsome income, and if we can get a handle on their spending, we should be able to help them achieve their financial goals. The financial plan will address each of the areas of concern individually.

Now let's look at the Moneymakers' net worth statement.

Net Worth Statement

Assets

Bank and Cash Account	5,000
Total Cash Assets	5,000

Other Assets

Rental Real Estate	350,000
Art Collection	100,000
Country Club Membership	45,000
Ben's Car	50,000
Sally's Car	35,000
Primary Residence	1,000,000
Total Other Assets	1,580,000

Investment Accounts

401(k) for Ben	332,350
401(k) for Sally	106,000
Brokerage Account	99,322
In-the-money Stock Options	98,634
Deferred Compensation	108,951
Total Investment Accounts	745,257

Total Assets	$2,330,257

Liabilities

Home Mortgage	850,000
Rental Property Mortgages	102,500
Credit Cards	10,000
Home Equity Line of Credit	55,000
Car Loans	60,000
Total Liabilities	$1,077,500

Net Worth (assets minus liabilities)	$1,252,757

While the Moneymakers' net worth is ample, their liquid position (things that can be readily converted to cash) is very, very skinny. First, as a basic rule of thumb, everyone should have at least three to six months of living expenses in cash at all times. The Moneymakers need more money market cash or cash in a checking account. Given their budget, they would need about $30,000 of liquid cash to meet our minimum recommendation. We will look for sources for that cash (the brokerage account with the aggressive stock losses comes to mind).

The Moneymakers also owe too much money for cars, and their mortgage payment is very steep. They may have an opportunity to refinance their mortgage at a much lower rate of interest. Since they are currently paying approximately 6.5 percent for a thirty-year fixed rate mortgage, we may be able to lower the payment almost $2,000 per month by looking to lower the interest rate to 5 percent on a five-year adjustable rate mortgage. We will make this recommendation and initiate a search for a competitive interest rate.

The next item that represents an opportunity for a higher revenue stream is the rental properties. Two opportunities exist here. The first is the income stream, which represents $850 monthly ($2,100 in rents minus the mortgages of approximately $1,250). The net effect of the rent is a return of slightly more than 2.9 percent (income of $10,200 per year divided by the properties' market value of $350,000). They may be able to increase this by increasing the rents. And second, we might refinance the rental properties at a lower rate of interest.

When looking at the assets on the net worth statement, a financial professional is looking for opportunities to increase revenue streams. When he or she looks at the liability side of the ledger, the opposite mind-set takes effect. Where can expenses be slashed to ease the burden on the cash flow? The mortgages and the opportunity to refinance demonstrate that mind-set. We can increase cash flow by raising rents and lowering interest payments.

The next asset problem is the cars. They must be very expensive if they are worth a combined $85,000. Keep in mind that this number represents market value. Therefore, you can presume that the Moneymakers paid more than that for the cars, which indicates a spending mentality that needs to be addressed. While it may be too late to alter the mind-set that produced the decision to buy cars they could not really afford, the opportunity to lower the monthly payment may still exist.

We can look at this scenario a couple of ways. One is to simply refinance the cars at a lower interest rate. Another way may be to look at the possibility of folding the car payment into the home equity line of credit. If they are paying 7 or 8 percent for the financing on the cars and they can borrow on the home equity line at 6 percent (and write off the interest), that may be worth examining. While we would never be anxious to increase debt levels, we would be interested in trading debt levels as we also acquire a tax advantage.

The next thing we have to address is the fact that the Moneymakers' net worth is substantial at a very young age. Generally that means they are going to have some estate tax issues down the road. Since they have to create a will anyway, it is probably in their interest to sit down with an estate attorney and figure out the best way to minimize the estate tax burden, which is likely to be a hefty amount upon the second death.

Assuming that we can fix their current financial situation, we can presume that their net worth at the age of sixty-five will be well past the Unified Tax Credit limit imposed by the government. For that reason we might suggest that they consider a wealth replacement trust or a second-to-die insurance policy in order for the executor to have the cash necessary to pay the estate taxes without having to sell an asset. However, the first step in that process will be to determine whether or not the Moneymakers care about paying taxes after their deaths.

I do not need to go into a detailed explanation of estate planning issues here. That is best left to an expert. But one thing bears reiteration, and that is how the Unified Tax Credit works. As I mentioned earlier, every citizen of the United States is allowed to accumulate a certain amount of assets during his or her lifetime that is exempt from federal estate tax. Currently, the amount is $1,000,000. However, this does not mean that a husband and wife automatically receive $2,000,000 worth of Unified Tax Credit. If a spouse dies and leaves everything to the other spouse, no estate taxes are due. That means that a spouse can leave tens of millions of dollars to the other spouse through the *unlimited marital deduction*. That's fabulous as far as it goes.

225

Let's imagine that happens. Ben dies and leaves $10,000,000 worth of assets to Sally without tax. Then Sally dies. Through the will, the estate deducts the unified credit of $1,000,000, which leaves a taxable estate of $9,000,000. The executor is going to have to write a check for approximately half that amount! Now, I don't know about you, but I think that would put a strain on any estate and any beneficiary who loses that money. By simple planning, the Moneymakers can create a family trust so that both spouses enjoy the extra million-dollar deduction. They can strategically invest some money while they are alive to provide the funds necessary to pay the taxes after they die. This is not a mandate, but it would be prudent, in my professional opinion.

The next priority has to be preparing for their children's college education. Unfortunately, they are too late for Justin, their oldest child, who is seventeen and ready to begin college. There is just no sensible or conservative method of investing over so short a time frame. By not preparing for this eventuality, Ben and Sally have forced themselves to fund the tuition through their current cash flow. However, we can try to soften that blow by enlisting the gifting opportunity available to the children's grandparents. Ben and Sally could approach their parents and request that they make a gift to Justin. Each grandparent can give away $10,000 to whomever they want each year as part of the Unified Tax Credit. Thus $40,000 per year might be available to the Moneymakers. We suggest doing this only if the gifts are worthwhile for the grandparents because the gifts help their estate tax situation, since their estates would be reduced by the amount of the gift. Obviously this would not be the situation for some grandparents.

Lest you think that $40,000 a year is enough, consider this. Based on 2003–2004 average costs, the estimated total cost for a student to attend private school for four years would be $153,916. A lump sum investment of $122,183 or an initial investment of zero with monthly investments of $3,910 would grow to $153,916. So the Moneymakers would have to set aside approximately $3,200 each month to finance Justin through college. Perhaps they can be convinced to forgo the private route and think about the public route. But that is not cheap either! Let's look at those numbers.

In 2003–2004 the estimated average total cost for a student to attend public school for four years was $72,073. That would take a lump sum investment of $57,214 or monthly investments of $1,831. In the case of the Moneymakers, about $100,000 is sitting in a stock account, which could be sold, given its aggressive nature and the advantages of taking the tax losses. That might be a place where we could go to tap the funds for the lump-sum investment. That determination would have to be made by the Moneymakers, but I would gladly trade the college education for the stock fund since doing so also removes the temptation for Mr. Moneymaker to continue to trade stocks and lose money unnecessarily.

Retirement Documents

ESTATE DOCUMENTS

The Moneymakers' wills are simple wills. If Ben dies, the money goes to Sally, and if Sally dies first, it all goes to Ben. The wills are out of date and do not include powers of attorney or living trusts. They must be rewritten.

RETIREMENT PLAN DOCUMENTS

First let's look at the LMN Savings Plan FBO Ben Moneymaker. FBO simply indicates "for benefit of," meaning that this is his 401(k).

Dodge & Cox Stock Fund	$ 25,300
Enhanced Stock Market	178,600
Montag & Caldwell Growth	114,000
Special Value	14,450
Total Value	$332,350

The ABC Savings Plan FBO Sally Moneymaker is simpler:

Company Stock	$106,000

My next step would be to take into account the existing positions within these savings plans to determine the Moneymakers' asset allocation and assess whether or not we want to make any changes. I will not go through the many details of this here.

Final Analysis

As a financial advisor, I face the tricky part in all of this in the way I deliver the message. Clearly the Moneymakers are successful people, so they may bristle when someone tells them anything that smacks of criticism. Yet this is precisely the role of the wise counselor.

Assuming the Moneymakers take my advice in the manner in which it is intended, we can go forward with a plan that strips away some of the spending. The first step in that process is a budget. You would be amazed at how much clearer financial problems become when seen in the glaring light of the printed page. I would ask the Moneymakers to write down everything they spend in a month, including with cash, and then categorize each expense. I would even have them mention the fifty cents they spend on chewing gum. "Do that for a month," I would say. "Then create an actual outline of your income and your expenses." The income side is easy. They simply add up their paychecks and rental income. The expense side is trickier, but possible. That exercise alone ought to wake them up to their destructive spending patterns.

Then I would redirect their saved expenditures into planned investing alternatives. Here's the hard part. Financial advisors can do much for you, but they cannot and will not police your spending or your consistent investing. I have never called a client and asked, "Hey, where's your check for the mutual fund this month?"

I truly hope that you don't recognize yourself in the Moneymakers' spending patterns and that you don't live beyond your means. That is the quickest way to misery that I know. Here are some of the key decisions that mid-lifers will need to address:

- children's college funding—cash flow or systematized investment program like a 529
- estate planning—are wills drawn and up to date? Do they reflect your desires?
- financial plan—can you see what the next thirty years look like financially?
- your parents' health concerns—perhaps look at long-term care insurance to protect against long nursing home contingencies
- likelihood of inheritances
- funeral plans for parents
- lessons learned from your parents which apply to your own situation

I always hesitate to be overly specific when discussing individual situations in a book. I want you to try to assimilate those things that may apply to your situation and discard the rest. But, if you take these ideas and apply them during your peak earning years, you can achieve your financial goals.

14

BILL AND VICKY ELDER

Investment Considerations for Retirees

We have seen a younger couple just starting out and a middle-aged couple trying to keep up with the Joneses. Now it's time to meet an older couple who have spent all of their lives trying to get to their golden years with some ammunition left in their six-guns.

Bill and Vicky Elder are in their late sixties, retired, and on a fixed income that includes a pension, an IRA, and Social Security.

In preparation for their interview, they've gathered their wills, brokerage and bank statements, details of pension payments, Social Security checks, insurance policies, certificates of deposit, bond holdings, detailed budget of monthly expenses, long-term care policy, and estate planning documentation.

Like many of my clients, Bill Elder began the interview by being explicit.

"As you can see, we aren't exactly spring chickens. We've been retired for a few years now, and we're concerned that we are going to outlive our money. Quite frankly, that scares the pants off us, since we don't want to be a burden to our children or grandchildren. We checked the prices of those assisted living places and glorified nursing homes. You wouldn't believe how expensive they are! We're wondering what happens to us down the road, so we figured we'd better see a professional."

"I appreciate your confidence in me. To do what you want, I have to ask you a bunch of rather personal questions. Will that be all right?"

"Fire away."

"Okay, first question. How old are you?"

"I'm sixty-eight," Bill replied. Vicky added, "I'm sixty-six."

"When did you retire?"

"We both retired two years ago," said Bill.

"Are you collecting Social Security?"

"Yes, we get about $2,100 each month."

"That's net?"

"Yes."

"Any other monthly income?"

"I get a pension from my company of $2,400 per month, and I'll get that for the rest of my life."

"What happens after you pass on?"

"My wife will get half of what I get until she dies."

"That's a pretty good deal."

"Yes, I worked for a great company for quite a while."

"Is that it as far as income streams?"

"Yes, although we do have some other investments . . . an IRA and things like that."

"All right, let's talk about those. How many IRAs do you have, and how much is in them?"

"I brought you the statement. There's only one, and it's worth $226,340 as of the last statement date. I have several individual stocks and a couple of mutual funds in there."

"Great. What about insurance? Do you have any annuities or any other investment insurance?"

"No."

"Okay, what about general life insurance?"

"I've got one little policy. I think it's a $50,000 whole life policy that's been paid up for quite a while. That's about it, though."

"So you are not making any payments on that now?"

"No. I think it has cash value, and they just take the premiums from that."

"What about cash? Do you have any cash sitting in checking, savings, or money markets?"

"Yes, I think we have about $17,000 or $18,000 in cash."

"Fine. Now, how much does it cost you to live each month?"

"I brought our budget. We pretty much spend what we take in, with a little left over. It's not much, though."

"Why is that? Do you still have a mortgage?"

"Yeah, we refinanced about a year ago and pulled some money out."

"What did you use that money for?"

"We bought a little place in the mountains. We go there during the summer to get out of the heat."

"What are your plans for the house you have here?"

"What do you mean?" Bill asked.

"Well, are you going to sell it in order to live in the mountains full time?"

"No, I don't think we want to do that. But we might sell it down the road if we have to go into assisted living or anything like that."

"What would you do with the mountain house then?"

"Well, we'd probably sell that as well."

"Okay, how much do you think the houses are worth?"

"Our house here would probably sell for $175,000, and the condo in the mountains might bring $75,000."

"How much is owed on the houses?"

"The condo is paid for. The house here has about $130,000 left on the mortgage."

"Other than housing, what's your biggest expense?"

"No question, it's health care. We pay about $800 a month for health care."

"Wow, that hurts!"

"Sure does, but it includes the Medicare supplement."

"Still pretty steep, but there really isn't any way around it; you have to have that coverage. . . . How is your health?"

"Fortunately, both of us are in pretty good shape. I've got a little high blood pressure."

"And I have arthritis," Vicki said. Then Bill added, "But other than that, we're pretty good."

"Come from long-lived families?"

"Not really. My dad died at seventy-three and my mother at seventy-six. I used to think that was pretty good until I hit sixty-five."

"My folks both died pretty young too," Vicky said.

"From what?"

"Both of my parents had cancer."

"And my dad died of a heart attack, my mother from emphysema," Bill added.

"Smokers?"

"Every one of them," Bill answered.

"Do you guys smoke?"

"Nope, neither one of us ever has."

"Good for you."

"How much does it cost you to live each month?"

"I have that right here. Let's see . . . about $2,750 per month."

"And your income is about $4,500 per month?"

"That's right."

"I don't see much of a problem. What's your concern?"

Vicki spoke immediately. "Well, if something happens to Bill, what happens to me?"

Now I knew where much of the concern was coming from. I answered her just as quickly to reassure her. "You would get half his pension and the greater of the Social Security payments. It would also cost you less to live since you would only have to provide for one person. I think you would be okay.

"The fly in the ointment is if you guys got sick and had to go into a nursing home. But even then we should be able to push enough money into income-producing vehicles with the real estate you have. Still, we need to check these things in order to make sure the numbers work."

"We have done some shopping around. Nursing homes, even marginal ones, cost a bunch. The ones we checked were something like $3,500 per month. For both of us, they were like five grand. Could we afford that with the assets we have?"

"I don't know until I run the numbers, but let's try to do a quick calculation. We already know that we have $4,500 coming in from various sources, so all you really need is another $500 from your investments each month. That's $6,000 per year, and I think you could comfortably get that from your IRA. With $225,000 or so in there, you would get $6,000 just by taking 3 percent out of that portfolio. So I think you are going to be fine. However, that doesn't relieve you of the responsibility to be prudent stewards of your assets. We need to also think about how to best position your assets in order to minimize taxes, maximize growth, and alleviate risk. So, let's take the proper approach and think about how to manage this money by determining what you want to happen to it once you pass on."

"We both would like it to go to our grandchildren." Vicky nodded in agreement and then added, "But only after our needs have been met."

"Your biggest fear is a prolonged stay in a nursing home?"

"For sure," Bill replied.

"Okay, so the first thing we have to do is ameliorate that fear by showing you in your financial plan that you have enough assets to cover that contingency. Once we do that, we can move on to the other areas of financial planning. Sound good?"

"Sure does. When will you get back to us?"

"Give us a week, okay?"

"Great."

The point of an initial interview is to figure out the most important financial problem facing the prospective clients. Clearly, Bill and Vicky Elder are worried about whether or not they can afford a nursing home. It seems to me that real progress cannot be made with the rest of their planning until that fear is gone. The fear is a little irrational in that they have plenty of assets with which to pay for a nursing home, given their healthy pensions (Social Security counts as retirement income). That doesn't matter. Until they believe they are secure, the fear is real. Remember the two prevailing emotions that kill financial decisions: fear and greed. They simply have to be identified and then addressed. In this case, it's pretty easy.

Converting the $225,000 that sits in Bill's IRA into a vessel from which he can withdraw $500 per month is really pretty simple. Since their need is slight (it's only about 2½ percent of the portfolio), we could invest some money in one of three options: United States Treasury bills, bonds, or notes. Then we easily get that yield without too much trouble.

However, in this case I think that's the wrong approach because Bill said they were afraid of outliving their money. For that reason, I will suggest a balanced approach. The first thing I would do is set aside $30,000 of the IRA in cash in a money market fund. That gives the Elders five years of living expenses should they need to go into an assisted living home. Even if they don't have to go into the nursing home, $30,000 is only slightly more than a 10 percent cash position within the IRA and probably prudent. I want to make certain they see cash sitting there, available for withdrawal, should they need it. That should go a long way toward calming their fears about income. Bill has to start withdrawing from his IRA in a couple of years anyway. (He's sixty-eight and has to withdraw by seventy-and-a-half.)

I think it is fairly common for folks of retirement age to draw some improper conclusions. For example, the Elders did some homework on nursing homes and figured a nursing home was going to cost $60,000 per year (true enough), and they only had $225,000 in Bill's IRA (also true). From there it was just a hop, skip, and a jump to decide they only had enough money to last about four years—not true at all! This kind of conclusion is really what Zig Ziglar, the famous motivational speaker, calls "stinking thinking."

Once again, we have our old friends fear and greed to thank for this amazing proclivity toward stinking thinking. The important lesson to be learned from the Elders and their misinterpretation of their financial situation is this: the need for growth in an investment portfolio never goes away, because even eighty-year-olds need to grow their money. That's why you can never completely give up on having a presence in the stock market. You just prune it back to match your risk tolerance and advancing age. The reasons can vary, but the need doesn't change. Of course, the reason has to do with the erosion of purchasing power over time.

The danger in structuring a portfolio for current income lies in the tendency to forget the need for growth. Most might think they need to convert *all* their assets to income-producing vehicles, and that's the mistake.

Remember those basic mistakes investors make from chapter 2? The failure to diversify was one of them. That's precisely the mistake older people make. They need to take care of their income need, no question. But they must not do it at the expense of asset allocation, since that provides the growth and minimizes the risk in the portfolio.

Let me illustrate it this way. Suppose we let the Elders use bonds in a fixed-income portfolio. The danger would be that they take all the money in Bill Elder's IRA and buy 6 percent non-investment grade bonds (with more risk in order to get higher interest). While the portfolio earns more than enough to pay his bills, the market value of the portfolio runs the risk of getting hammered if interest rates rise. That could increase Bill and Vicky's fear and cause them to sell the bonds at a needless, perhaps substantial, loss. What initially looked great on paper can have disastrous consequences because of the lack of diversification. I've seen it happen many, many times.

Let me give you a real-life situation. A retired business-man and his wife came to me several years ago. They didn't like their broker and wanted to "do better." We spent all the appropriate time in interviews and determined together that we needed to broaden the diversity in their portfolio. They had a reliance on fixed income and not nearly enough in growth vehicles, so we diversified into growth mutual funds while setting aside a healthy dose of cash in order to provide the monthly income they needed for a couple of years. By doing that, we gave the growth portion of the portfolio some time before they needed more income.

Well, as luck would have it, we made a lot of money very, very quickly due to the stock market taking off. It became apparent that we needed to take some of those profits in order to lessen the risk (we now had too much in growth due to appreciation). We did that and broadened the diversification even further.

We then met with the man and his wife to suggest that the portfolio was still too aggressive. We advised taking a fair amount of the portfolio and converting it into even more cash; however, we still maintained a hefty amount of the portfolio in growth mutual funds spread across large cap, mid cap, small cap, and international funds.

Sure enough, the market went down significantly. One day I was notified that the couple had called my assistant and sold everything. I called them to stop this change, but to no avail. They thought they were going to lose all their money. A few weeks later I got a notice saying that they were transferring their accounts. Had the couple simply held onto their portfolio and allowed us to manage their fear through the difficult market, they would have enjoyed handsome gains.

However, the result was a double whammy in that the couple lost money twice needlessly. They lost when they sold out of the market too soon, and they lost by being out of the market during the recovery. Quite frankly, that would be my concern about the Elders.

In a real-life setting, we'd also go over the Elders' budget and net worth statement in depth, but I'd rather not bore you with the details here. The Elders have enough assets to solve their financial problem, and their cash flow is adequate, given some minor tweaking. They just need to resolve their fear of the future. Financial planning can be a necessary help at any age.

15

A FINAL EXAMINATION

Our Fictional Couples, Your Life, and Mine

The malady afflicting the Youngpersons, the Moneymak-ers, and the Elders emanates from their hearts. Even though one might argue that they all appear to be nice, honest, hard-working people, I would argue that something also appears to be missing. A careful re-reading of their interviews reveals the answer. I would ask the young couple who wanted to retire at fifty, "Why do you want to retire so early?" My guess would be that the Youngpersons think this represents the good life. You don't have to work anymore, you get to play golf every day—or do whatever you are looking to do to fill the hours. I would bet that the Youngpersons don't really know why they want to retire so young. They just think that's part of the American dream.

The Moneymakers' problem is obvious. They suffer from the love of money, and we all know what the Bible has to say about that.

As for the Elders, their issue lies in fear.

My point in all of this is that all three couples have the wrong focus. The dilemma for me as a financial advisor is getting people to understand that they need to lift their eyes toward heaven and away from their bank balances. This is easier said than done, and it's my prime motivation for writing this book.

I believe the answer lies in the heart. As long as mortals seek answers in the stuff of this world, the problem will continue. In chapter 10 I said that nothing in this world belongs to us. We are merely stewards temporarily in charge of the blessings bestowed upon us by our Creator. We need to be grateful for those blessings whatever their size or importance. Furthermore, we need to be aware of the awesome responsibility inherent in those blessings. Since the blessings are really a loan from God to us, we should recognize that we need to pay him back with interest! We need to be good stewards.

Remember the passage I mentioned in chapter 10? It was Malachi 3:8–10, my favorite passage in the Bible. God required the Israelites—and us—to give him the first 10 percent of all they made. Then God said the most amazing thing. He told his children that if they would not rob him of the tithe, he would pour out a blessing upon them that they would not believe. And he *even guaranteed it!* If you don't believe me, try me, God said. Isn't that amazing? God made a deal: You give me back 10 percent of what I gave you, and you get to keep the other 90 percent. If you do that, I will pour out a blessing upon you that you won't believe.

I don't know about you, but I think that's a pretty good deal.

Truth be told, that passage is the secret of financial planning. To all those people who come to me with problems they think may be insurmountable, I offer the following advice: *tithe*.

To all those people who think they are one paycheck away from the poorhouse, I offer the following advice: *tithe*.

To all those people who think bankruptcy is their only alternative, I offer the following advice: *tithe*.

To all those people whose phones ring off the hook with collection agencies demanding payment on their over-extended credit cards, I offer the following advice: *tithe*.

I can offer true-life stories of situations where that advice has eased the burden that seemed impossible days before.

A young couple in my home group Bible study came to me in tears. They had just had their first child, the husband had lost his job, and they owed over $20,000 in credit card debt. They had no savings and no prospects to earn any more cash. What should they do? "Tithe," I said.

"But we can't afford it," they said.

"You can't afford not to," I said. "Tithe."

They did. What happened next is the most amazing story of all. A week later the husband got a job paying $6,000 more in salary than his previous job, and the wife's parents paid off the couple's credit cards because her folks believed that tithing demonstrated the right spirit.

Or consider the minister's wife who withdrew $500 from an ATM machine for monthly expenses. On her way home she saw a homeless man begging on the street and gave him the $500. No questions asked. He needed it. She gave it to him. Or should I say, she gave it to God! The next day a check arrived for, you guessed it, $500!

Now, if a lot of this sounds like just so much hocus-pocus, then we need to work on more than your finances.

What is it that you believe about your finances? In short, I want to know if you are the problem. Has someone done something to you to cause your financial problems, or are you the culprit?

Now, this is going to demand some rather searing honesty on your part. I have come to realize that most people (if they are honest) recognize that they are the problem and the source of their financial misery. They spent money they didn't have. They didn't work as hard as they should have. They looked to themselves for financial insight when they had none. They could not trust. There are literally hundreds of reasons for financial failure.

Here's what I have come to learn from twenty years, much pain, and hundreds of thousands of dollars in losses: when it was up to me, I fouled it up. I suspect, after much introspection and study, that C. S. Lewis was right when he wrote in *Mere Christianity* that the worst sin is pride. In order for financial success to get easier, one has to kill one's pride and trade the earthly life for glorious eternal life. That does not mean that earthly financial success is forbidden in the Christian world. Hardly! The Lord wants us to have life and have it abundantly. We will each explain what we did with his bounty on judgment day. But the point is that there can be bounty!

So let me leave you with one last story. Two years ago, I got fired as the co-host of a morning radio program in Charlotte. It was a good job and provided a handsome paycheck. The station wanted me to stay and do a weekend financial show. I still had a year and a half on my contract that they would have to pay whether I stayed or not.

I spent six weeks in conversation with the Lord. "What do you want me to do, Lord?" I asked. "Do you want me to stay on the radio on that station and do a weekend financial show? Is that how you want me to serve you?"

What came back was not a simple no in answer to my question. What I heard the Lord say was, "NO WAY!"

Honest. It was that startling and that clear. So I said, "Okay, Lord, what do you want me to do?"

The answer to that question was similar to Jesus's reply to the rich young man who asked what he had to do to get into heaven (see Luke 18:18–27). Jesus told him to follow the Ten Commandments. Okay, the rich young ruler said, I've done that—and I will continue to do so.

Then Jesus, knowing that the young man was very rich and that money was his god, said, "Then sell everything you have and follow me." Sadly, the young man could not do this; instead he just faded back into the crowd.

Well, I heard the Lord give me the same answer, with a couple of extra little goodies added.

"Quit your job at that New York Stock Exchange firm you currently work for," he said, "and start up another one with my Son at the center of it. Get off that radio show and start your own network. But I don't want you preaching to the choir. I want you to syndicate that show throughout the United States to a secular audience so that you can use the talents I have given you to be a light in a very dark world. Then I want you to give speeches and write books telling people how to use the blessings I have bestowed upon them in a manner pleasing to me. Oh, and one more thing. Sell everything you have and put it behind all of the things I just told you to do."

That's what he said. I heard him.

And so I did it.

What transpired after that has been eye-opening to say the least. I put all of my money behind the new endeavors, but I still needed to raise additional funds to adequately capitalize everything the Lord told me to do. When I went into the secular world to raise this money, almost everybody told me the same thing: "You can't do it. One man can't do all that. It's impossible. If you bring faith into your radio show, people will be offended. You can't do it. It won't work."

The amazing thing is that I completely agreed with everything they said. I knew I couldn't do it. The problem was trying to get other people to understand that *I* wasn't doing it. *God* was doing it, and they couldn't convince me that he couldn't do it. I knew he could do anything. So all that remained was for people to get out of God's way.

The brokerage firm called Triune Capital Advisors, LLC, started in September of 2004, and "The Danny Fontana Show" on the Charis Network is syndicated Monday through Friday throughout the United States. I give lots of speeches and speak frequently in churches throughout the country. I wrote this book. All of these enterprises are dedicated to funneling profits into God's work.

I had absolutely, positively nothing to do with any of it. He did it all.

May God bless each of you in the same way.

Appendix

Net Worth Worksheet

Assets:

	Cash	_____
	Mutual Funds	_____
	Savings Bonds	_____
	401(k)	_____
	SEP IRA	_____
	Home	_____
	Autos	_____
Total Assets		_____

Liabilities:

	Car Loans	_____
	Other Debts	_____
	Rent or Mortgage	_____
Total Liabilities		_____

Total Assets	_____
minus Liabilities	– _____
Net Worth	$_____

Monthly Budget Worksheet

Income:

	Salary	_____
	Salary	_____
Total Income		_____

Expenses

	Income Tax (28 percent)	_____
	Rent or mortgage payment	_____
	Food	_____
	Car payments	_____
	Phone	_____
	Cable	_____
	Utilities	_____
	Entertainment	_____
	Clothing	_____
	Miscellaneous	_____
Total Expenses		_____

Potential Savings (income minus expenses)   _____

NOTES

Chapter 4: What Goes Around Comes Around

1. Jordan Goodman, *Everyone's Money Book* (Chicago: Dearborn Financial Publishing, 1997), 50.

Chapter 6: I Double Dog Dare You

1. R. G. Ibbotson Associates, Inc., *The Stocks, Bonds, Bills, and Inflation Yearbook* (Silver Spring, MD: CDA Investment Technologies, Inc., 1985).
2. Ibid.
3. Ibid.

Chapter 9: Two Things Are Certain

1. Goodman, *Everyone's Money Book*, 641.
2. Greenwich Associates, Greenwich, Connecticut.

Chapter 10: All That Stuff—It's Not Really Yours

1. *Webster's Ninth New Collegiate Dictionary*, s.v. "stewardship."
2. James P. Lenfestey, "Catch of a Lifetime," as found in Gordon MacDonald, *When Men Think Private Thoughts* (Nashville: Nelson, 1997), 243-44.

Backed by twenty years of experience in the financial services industry, **Danny Fontana** hosts the nationally syndicated *Danny Fontana Show* on the Charis Network and Inspirational Life Television (i-Lifetv). The founder and CEO of Triune Capital Advisors, Danny is a stockbroker and a frequent speaker for numerous Fortune 500 companies. Married, the father of three, and the grandfather of four, he lives in Charlotte, North Carolina.